Jesus, Save Me
from Your
Followers

Jesus, Save Me from Your Followers

Confessions of a Confused Leader!

Dave Gilpin

New Wine Press

New Wine Ministries
PO Box 17
Chichester
West Sussex
United Kingdom
PO19 2AW

ISBN 1–903725–72–0

Typeset by CRB Associates, Reepham, Norfolk
Cover design by CCD, www.ccdgroup.co.uk
Printed in Malta

Contents

Preface

Your future is bigger than your past. This book is dedicated to a new breed of leader who is prepared to re-think and challenge all that's gone before in order to reinvent themselves for the greater things that lie ahead.

Leadership in the 21st Century is different from the leadership of any other century, including that of the past ten years. Why? Because we live in a rapidly changing world where the cutting edge leadership that was in demand a decade ago may not be cutting it today.

Who said that being a "controlling" leader was wrong? Is "control" such a bad thing? Who said that charisma and personality were non-essentials in the building of the Church and that all we needed was great teaching and deep truth? Who told you that "the sky's the limit" and who invented the term "servant-leader"? In all of my travels I've never heard of a "front of plane" pilot and never seen a pilot sitting at the back of a plane! Who told you that you needed to be everybody's friend and to never show favouritism to anyone in your team or ministry? Firstly, who said you needed a team anyway?

The majority of church leaders are secretly confused, but never admit to it. To that end I've decided to shed some light onto many of those areas where leaders feel most confused and to spill the beans on the real struggle of being a Christian leader on the cutting edge. At the end of each chapter I've included my "Diary Archives" which will, I hope, give an insight into the highs and lows, successes and failures, joys and disappointments that are the stock in trade of every leader. It's time to confess and be real!

It's also time to rethink. It's time to step aside from the general consensus of Jesus' followers and reignite the gift of leadership. In the light of the shifting culture in which we live, it's our time to create a leadership that will take our ministries and our churches into new heights of effectiveness and growth. Care to join me?

Dave Gilpin
Senior Pastor
Hope City Church
England

Introduction

God is brilliant – it's just His people I have trouble with! Despite all its ups and downs, Christian leadership should be bottled and shipped out to every one of the world's organisations, both big and small – our workforce is purely voluntary, we trade in the invisible, and we're always up against the impossible!

If you're a Christian leader, I salute you! You're already doing better than you think you're doing! *Jesus, Save Me from Your Followers* has been written to encourage you to go further and to fly higher on the journey of leadership you've embarked upon.

Who was the greatest Briton that ever lived? Was it Churchill or Wesley? Wilberforce or Brunel? In a recent survey the people of Britain voted for Churchill, not only because of his integrity, but also because he soared in a gift that lives deep within every one of us – the gift of great leadership. His gift didn't gather dust; it was wielded in both hands, enabling him to take a great cause and from it create a great outcome.

They say that leaders are neither born nor made. Leaders are people who choose to rise up in adversity and determine the outcome of their circumstances. They lead the way; others follow. If you could do anything knowing you simply could not fail, what would it be? If it's part of God's dream for your life, the bridge between where you are right now and where you'd like to be lies in this gift – the gift of leadership.

This book is for everyone who really wants to excel in leadership. It's for everyone who knows that the greatest cause on planet earth is the expansion of the Church, and the greatest way to see this happen is through maximising the gift of leadership. It's a book for ministers, core team leaders, supporting leaders and emerging leaders. Underpinning every-thing is a passion to move the Church, your church, into the 21st Century and to get you rethinking theories and practices that have been considered "gospel" in the Christian world.

The book of Nehemiah gives us four pre-requisites that need to be fulfilled right at the beginning of the journey of leadership:

The first is to ask probing questions!

When Nehemiah heard that men had returned from his homeland, he questioned them in detail, both about the state of the people and about the area they had visited. Many people say and do things just because they have heard other people say and do them. Leaders ask the hard questions – not cynically, but intelligently. They want, and need, the low-down to prepare for the up-rise. Leaders don't simply accept the status quo; they study how to change it.

The second prerequisite is to be faithful and get passionate!

They say that if you're faithful to someone else's dream, God will give you your own. Not true! Unless you truly own someone else's dream and make it yours, not a lot will happen with that dream, or any other dream you may have. Nehemiah became governor of Jerusalem after he was cupbearer to the king of Persia. To become cupbearer to the king you've got to be a great cupbearer. Before he was even a cupbearer he must have been an awesome kitchen hand in downtown Babylon. Faithfulness leads to positions that require great faith.

It's time to sink your teeth into the vision surrounding your church, your workplace, your studies and the lives of others. Don't just serve. Get into it with a passion. Let the gift arise now, not just for a future time.

The third prerequisite that needs to be fulfilled is to find a problem and solve it!

If George Biro hadn't had a problem with the fountain pen he would never have invented the first ballpoint pen. Had the Fourth Earl of Sandwich not had a problem with sit-down lunches he would have never invented the sandwich. Trouble is a doorway to advancement. Nehemiah saw a dilapidated city and said, "With God's help, I can do something about that." Paul said that his troubles were achieving eternal glory for him that he would one day see. It's time to add prayer and wisdom to our troubles to turn our problems into opportunities. The journey of leadership begins with a problem that no one else is solving – it's been left for you.

The last thing that's needed to begin the journey of leadership is to simply get started!

Nehemiah wasn't invited to become a leader; he got motivated and others followed. If you see a vacuum, fill it. Take the incentive. No one asked me to write a book – I did it anyway. No one asked our church to do a Night of Honour for the City of Sheffield – we did it anyway. No one's asking any of us to build a great church or business. Do it anyway! Your world awaits you. Let the gift arise!

Nehemiah *was asked*, however, how long it would take and when he would get back. Stop procrastinating and start noting in your diary everything that needs to be done. Get the ball rolling!

Every gift in every heart is released by the gift of leadership. When the incredibly talented Robbie Williams got caught in a downward spiral of drugs and disillusionment Guy Chambers came along, sorted out his life, and released his talent in singing. Together they have created musical history. Without Guy Chambers there would be no Robbie Williams. Without Alex Ferguson there would be no David Beckham. And without Sue Gentle (my University friend who introduced me to Christ), there would be no Dave Gilpin. Someone took the lead and created the future. The world awaits your leadership. The future of the Kingdom waits for you to arise!

PS: Every book on leadership can leave people feeling like they're miles away from where they should be on the road of leading others into their future destiny. Because of that I've included extracts from my "warts and all" diary. It begins two years after a season of great upheaval (that's an understatement!) in my life and ministry and concludes three years later at the onset of a great season of growth and vitality that has continued to this day! Enjoy watching me suffer.

It's Not the Winning or the Taking Part That Counts

The Confusion of Vision

Vision is everything. Your inner eyes of faith are your link between what is and all that will be! It's the role of every leader to "see" with the eyes of faith, to "declare" what they see to the people around them, and to keep on going until they see it come to pass. Your vision determines your future.

It's rare to find a leadership book that doesn't dedicate at least a chapter to the subject of vision. In most cases, however, it's associated only with goals and aspirations. Most leaders think that vision casting is all about telling people what they'll be up to in five years' time and what projects will have come to pass. They've been unwittingly backed into a corner.

In this chapter we're going to look at what vision is really about and we're going to redefine what real success actually is, so that all you declare as a leader can be both accessible and achievable!

Redefining vision

Vision is the motivating force behind everything we do. You can never say to someone, "Let's motivate ourselves," because motivation is simply a by-product of the transference of vision. If I can "see" something great I'll do anything I can to see it come to pass. Vision gives birth to commitment, enthusiasm, energy and discipline.

Because of its intoxicating influence many leadership books have gone to town on it with the premise: "If you can believe it, you'll one day see it!" The huge problem with that is that you can't make yourself believe anything. Either you believe it or you don't. Either God said it or He didn't. You can't half believe and you can't make yourself believe. Either the conviction is there or it's not.

There is a big, big pressure on leadership to have to come up with magnificent plans and huge goals in order to be the "visionary" leader that they've been reading about. In doing so, many overstep the boundaries of faith and move into the big world of presumption, where everyone is now "trying" to believe. They begin to lead people into "big disappointment" territory that many followers never recover from.

Many leaders think that if they were really "spiritual" they'd hear God's voice more accurately regarding the details of their future and what will actually be taking place from one year to the next. It's the absence of "hearing" (as well as the huge pressure from the gurus of vision) that causes a lot of leaders to panic and tag on "the Lord said" to their goals and dreams – when He never actually said anything.

The problem doesn't lie in the spirituality of the leader, however, it lies in the absence of details when God actually does speak to us! The overwhelming majority of words spoken by God to us are about a revelation of His nature, not His plans! To Jeremiah, God declared, *"For I know the plans I have for you . . . plans to prosper you and not to harm you, plans to give you a hope and a future"* (Jeremiah 29:11). God knew the fine print but wasn't about to talk about it. Instead, He revealed the nature of the future (prosperous and good), not the details of the future. The nature of the future was a direct imprint of the nature and character of God. Vision, therefore, has less to do with what people will be doing in five years' time and more to do with the spirit they'll be carrying in five years' time!

My role as a visionary leader isn't primarily to declare where we'll all be in three years' time, but to declare what we'll all be like. God's word is much more to do with "culture creation" than goal setting and tangible accomplishments. God knows that creating a climate of the revelation knowledge of Himself is the hothouse from which all growth will come. Our principal goal is really to do with the people who are following us – that they would see, become like, draw close to, and do the business of God.

The language of hope

While some leaders have extrapolated God's word, declaring things that He never actually said, others have sat back, waiting for that amazing word of faith to fall from heaven regarding the details of the future. When it eventually comes they'll do something about it; but in the meantime, they'll just wait!

Whether God has spoken or whether God hasn't spoken, the lives of leaders should be filled with the spirit of faith that results in what I call, "the language of hope".

When confronting the Philistine's outpost (1 Samuel 14:6) Jonathan did not say to his armour bearers, "The Lord will act on our behalf"; he said, *"Perhaps the LORD will act ... "* He exercised the language of hope. He knew that, *"nothing can hinder the LORD from saving, whether by many or by few."* That word was a definitive word about the nature, character and ability of his God. His use of the word "perhaps" was based on his word of faith, but wasn't itself a word of faith – it was the language of expectancy, but not certainty.

It's essential that we are confident, but not overconfident, in our leadership. It's important that we promise, but not over promise. We all need to lighten up and say to the people who are following us, "Why don't we just give it a go? It's a noble task and it's possible that we just might succeed!" In doing so, we create people who are less hung up on a word of faith and more consumed by the spirit of faith. We create a "yes" culture where it's a "yes" until God says "no"; it's a green light unless we see a red light.

In Paul's letter to the Colossians he writes, *"Let the peace of Christ rule in your hearts . . . "* (Colossians 3:15). The Greek word for "rule" has the overtone of someone acting as an umpire. Umpires don't tell you when to kick and where to kick, they tell you when you're out, offside and out of bounds. Players don't watch the umpire when they play; they simply keep one ear open to the umpire. Christian living has already been given a whistle to go, but every now and then there comes the sound of a whistle when play is to be stopped. So many Christians, for example, pray about how much to give when it comes to an offering or an opportunity to be generous, yet the right thing for them to do is to go ahead and give and listen out for when to stop! Ecclesiastes 11:6 says,

> "Sow your seed in the morning,
>   and at evening let not your hands be idle,
> for you do not know which will succeed,
>   whether this or that,
>   or whether both will do equally well."

For a lot of leaders that is too vague for their style of leadership. It is, however, excellent leadership. I'm ninety percent sure that we're going to succeed in all that we're doing as a church. The ten percent isn't "leaving room for doubt", it's leaving room for the ways of God that He never spoke to me about.

I've learned to be comfortable in being "faithless", but I'm ruthless with unbelief. Faithlessness is simply the absence of hearing a specific word from God. It shouldn't slow you down as you proceed in the spirit of faith with the language of hope. Unbelief, however, is the refusal to agree with what you actually heard when God spoke into your heart. The two are poles apart. When you understand the difference, it can make you very confident in saying, "I'm not sure"; "I don't know" and "let's give it a go". It heavily reduces the fallout if what you attempt to do doesn't come to pass. Everyone's up for it again when you attempt another project because they've learnt to live in the spirit of faith. Short-term failure isn't such a big deal because, in the long run, God's plans to make us prosper and multiply will find their way into our life and ministry.

Here are some expressions that are a part of the great language of hope:

- "Where did it all start to go so right?"
- "What's the best that can happen?"
- "You just don't know what a new day will bring."
- "How come I get all the luck!"

I recently wrote an article for our church magazine that is a good example of my leadership gift and the language of hope at work. I provocatively called it, "I should be so lucky". It's upbeat, focuses on attitude and spirit and doesn't promise anything that is inaccessible to anyone following me.

> Goodbye "living by chance"! Hello "living by the favour of heaven"! If you live by chance – bad luck! If you live by the favour of heaven – all luck to you. The 23rd Psalm is being

outplayed before you right now – the Lord leading you beside still waters and green pastures . . . the Lord right there with you in every shadowy valley . . . His powerful rod and staff always surrounding you. Everyone, and I mean everyone, who puts their faith in Jesus Christ can expect the 23rd Psalm, twenty-four-seven.

Many people associate luck with things like their numbers coming up on Saturday night or some long lost rich relative dying and giving them some of their inheritance. For the Christian, their luck is very different from that. It's everywhere. It's in God's promises; it's in the good times; it's in our connections with people; and it's just beneath the surface in the "bad" times. Even when stuff hits the fan, you can scoop all of that stuff up to create the most incredible of gardens. Even when the early disciples were jailed and then sent before the law lords they thought it "lucky" that they should be considered "worthy" of suffering for Jesus. The Bible is full of references to the "favour" of God. When you're favoured you become very lucky! Jesus grew both in favour with people and favour with heaven. You can grow in that favour too. Just as a recording artist can do well in more than one country at one time, you too can grow in favour inwardly, outwardly and influentially. Here are three ways to grow in "luck":

▶ *Decide to believe.* After Mary heard the news about her immaculate conception, her cousin Elizabeth said to her, "Blessed is she who believes what the Lord has said to her will come to pass." "Blessed" is an old fashioned word that actually means, "happy, fortunate and to be envied". It really means, "incredibly lucky". Mary was favoured because she believed. In other words, positive outcomes abound to those who decide to put their faith in Jesus. (You can't make yourself believe, but you can align yourself with your believing.)

▶ **Decide to delight.** Psalm 1:1–3 says, *"Blessed is the man who*[se] *... delight is in the law of the* LORD *... He is like a tree planted by streams of water..."* There it is again – blessed. Incredibly lucky is the person who lets their excitement abound in their walk with God. Your excitement attracts the favour of heaven. "I'm loving it" isn't just for people who love Big Macs, it's for people who want to excel in the favour of heaven.

▶ **Decide to stick it out.** Psalm 84:5 says, *"Blessed are those whose strength is in you, who have set their hearts on pilgrimage."* Pilgrimage is all about the journey of life; not just the events of life. Those who decide to do the journey with God are very lucky people. Luck isn't always getting what you want. In fact, if you're lucky, you'll realise that what you want isn't always what you really, really want. God doesn't just have today in mind, but the whole of your future in His view. A twelve-year-old with car keys isn't lucky, but an eighteen-year-old with the same keys *is* lucky. God's a builder, not a gambler. He doesn't gamble with today in spite of tomorrow. Sometimes difficulties are bits of luck in disguise. Great difficulties produce great character and great character is the foundation of great dreams. I told you that you were lucky!

Why settle for touching wood when you can touch heaven itself and watch your life grow in grace and favour causing everyone around you to think, "Why should you be so lucky?" (You can't make yourself believe, but you can align yourself with your believing.)

What I love about this article is its visionary and cheeky nature. It's written to stir people into a new way of seeing. It is triumphant in spirit, yet not triumphalistic. It has anchors that earth the message back to where people are at, yet it has a huge updraft that is free of the cynicism and doubt that plague so many people in our churches. It is a message written, not by an observer, but by a leader. It casts a vision, but it's a vision of spirit, not a vision of detail. We're embarking on a zillion plans, but my vision is rooted, not in the plans, but the spirit behind the plans!

Redefining success

In order to create a vision that's achievable and liveable it's also vital that you redefine what true success actually is. God promised prosperity and success to Joshua, but what does success mean to 21st Century Christian leaders? People used to say, "It's not the winning that counts, it's the taking part!" We then said, "It's not the taking part that counts, it's the winning!"

Both these expressions hold truth, but neither is the absolute truth. Why? Because we're not called to win, we're called to succeed! There's a big difference between winning and succeeding. You can succeed, but not win. Christopher Reeve may not have been considered for the part of Spiderman after being crippled from the neck down, but his story is one of success; of a man who kept fighting and believing despite incredible odds.

To build a "success" culture is one of the greatest mandates upon the life of a leader. If you build a "success" culture you can live in it twenty-four-seven.

If you aim only to win you'll find that getting silver means only one thing – you lost. It follows then, that if you're busy creating a "winning" culture, you will automatically create a "losing" culture, because only one can win in any race and at any one time. If you create a "success" culture you can produce an attainable and multipliable culture that can succeed all of the time.

Ten "seconds" to successful leadership

If you look through the Bible you'll find that second comes first every time. Here are ten "seconds" to create a success culture that produces highly successful churches and people that take the kingdom of heaven by force. For them, to win is neither here nor there; to succeed is paramount.

1. Second place

After sharing His parable about a day in the life of a vineyard, Jesus declared the classic line, *"The last will be first, and the first will be last"* (Matthew 20:16). Those who came early and chose to work in the vineyard for a set fee got what they bargained for. Those who were chosen later in the day, who agreed to work for "whatever was right", got much more per hour than those who came early. Those who put themselves first, in fact, came last. Those who put themselves second actually ended up coming first.

Church division is rarely caused by the churches that are "top of the league" for numbers, at the cutting edge for media, leading the way in music and are the most popular. They're more often caused by church leaders who have fostered a "winning" culture, wishing in their hearts that they could be leading one of "those" types of churches. A success culture doesn't despise those who "win" – it either honours them or ignores them. Suspicion, judgement, gossip and whining, however, are all fostered by a spirit of intimidation that is engendered by a "win–lose" culture. To succeed is to "honour one another above yourself" and to always choose to want others to do as well as, if not better, than you have ever done. Coming second comes first every time! A truly successful culture will cause each person to "run the race" marked out for them, without the trappings of competition, inferiority or pride.

2. Second fiddle

Aaron played second fiddle to Moses, Jonathan to David and John to Peter. Every other conference nowadays is a "Leadership and Emerging Leaders" conference – not necessarily to raise up leaders, but definitely to boost attendance! No one likes a "how to follow" conference and few visit www.armlifters.com even though they ought to! Our dream should always incorporate the fulfilment of someone else's dream so much so that it becomes our own.

Benjamin Zander, in his excellent book, *The Art of Possibility*,[1] talks about the symptoms of those who suffer from "second fiddle-itus". In his role of conducting The Boston Symphony Orchestra for over twenty years, he's seen them many times over.

Firstly, it's a loss of significance. Second violins can see themselves simply as redundant foot soldiers. Does anyone really hear them or care? Secondly, it's a loss of enthusiasm. Practise dwindles and tuning is less refined. Thirdly, it is a loss of excellence; the last to arrive – the first to leave.

Zonder believes that the second fiddles actually rule the roost – they actually come first. They determine inner rhythms and harmonies and establish the driving authority and clarity of the piece of music. They drive the music.

Behind every soloist in church life is a band of second violins. They are like the pillars of a building – never truly exalted, rewarded, fully noticed or appreciated – yet the church is built on them. Build a success culture that creates incredible second fiddles, fully free from "second fiddle-itus". Exalt the "unsung heroes" and you'll multiply your leadership effectiveness.

3. Second mile

Remember Jesus' parable about giving to those who ask? In the first mile they had your tunic, but you still had your cloak.

In the second mile you had neither tunic nor cloak. The second mile, however, always leads to the promised third mile. "Give and it shall be given, pressed down..." A winning culture walks only one mile until real loss becomes imminent. A success culture loses its life for others in the knowledge that with every seed sown lies a potential harvest to share again.

The reason so many churches don't fully excel is that they have some kind of nest egg in reserve. People stay in the personal comfort of the first mile. You've got to be exhausted to be recharged, empty to be refilled, and bereft to be restored! Dirt is good when it is filled with the seeds of generosity. Brown soon turns to gold. We need to lead people past the first mile, through the second and into the third!

4. Second wind

Be strong, endure hardship, serve as a soldier, be a hardworking farmer etc., etc., etc. It's all there – the challenge to break the "Law of Hard". It's a law so many live within which prevents them from getting their second wind. The Law of Hard is expressed through sentiments like, "It's too hard," "I can't go on" and "I can hardly cope." No athlete gets their second wind until they break through the pain barrier. For the Christian, the pain barrier often represents the fixed line between human and heavenly strength.

The second wind is the wind of the Spirit filling the sails of someone who has finally nailed their colours to the mast: "Not my will be done, but Yours." To come second to the one who is "The First" and "The Last", by the surrender of our will is to create a success culture that's filled with gusts from heaven blowing us into our destiny. Don't ever allow the "it's hard" culture to seep into all that you do. It will kill the success.

5. Second chance

"Then the word of the LORD *came to Jonah a second time..."*
(Jonah 3:1). A winning culture becomes a culture only for the
strong and the young. A success culture is a culture that gives
every person a fighting chance of achieving great things. To
succeed is to often admit you've failed, but to never brand
yourself a failure.

The truth is that the second chance has a much better chance
than the first chance – that's why heaven's full of them. It may
have been that godly opportunity was met by ambition and
human arrogance. To have succeeded on the first go would
have fed the "monster" within with terrible consequences.
To have "blown it" and come back is to again meet godly
opportunity, this time with "poverty of spirit", producing
the perfect combination. As Oswald Chambers puts it, "The
knowledge of our own poverty brings us to the mortal frontier
where Jesus Christ works." Jesus Christ is currently trading in
church-building, soul-saving, disciple-making opportunities at
the isolated outpost where faith meets brokenness. It's the
"second chance" saloon. It reeks of real and substantiated
success. It's the training ground of great leadership.

6. Second half

When Roy Riggles took the ball at the Rose Bowl College final,
he ran with all his might. Upon touchdown, instead of cheering,
the crowds went silent and a cold wind blew over the stadium.
He'd run the wrong way. Coach Price tried to console Roy
at half time, but with no success. "Same team second half as
first half" was, to Roy, a poor decision. Roy didn't move. Coach
Price leant over and declared to Roy, "The game is only half
over." The next day the papers declared that Roy Riggles
played the second half like a man possessed.

You need to give birth to a Manasseh ("forgetting what is

behind") before you give birth to your Ephraim ("fruitful in the land of your suffering"). Right now, the second half, the greatest half of your ministry life, lies in front of you. Leadership capitalises on the power of a new day. It puts history in the vaults of the past and moves on into the second phase. It faces forward and develops a memory for the future, not the past.

7. Second opinion

"Plans fail for lack of counsel, but with many advisors they succeed" (Proverbs 15:22). A winning culture often neglects to ask around as it soars off to reach for the skies. A success culture is filled with second opinions from "reliable men" only. Don't ask a novice; what do they know? And don't ask Mr Long-in-the-Tooth who still has nothing to show for himself. Ask Mr Fruitful and Mrs Proven. A third opinion though could possibly be the scent of procrastination. Don't ask for too many opinions. Too many cooks always contradict each other and spoil the broth. Great leadership knows when to ask and when to make a final decision to move on or to stop.

8. Second nature

Once you've learnt how to ride a bike it becomes second nature. You can do it forever. Once a musician has practised and practised an arpeggio, it becomes second nature; they can play it with their ears shut. You always need to move on from first nature to second. Romans 12 asks us to be changed by the renewing of our minds. When revelation hits our spirit (producing faith), it creates a pathway of thought within the mind. We can see it. It's our job then to change that pathway into a four-lane freeway! We need to discipline our thinking to constantly line up with our inner revelation. We need to create trains of thought that widen the pathway until it becomes a highway of "second nature thinking". Only then, Paul says, can we experience God's *"good, pleasing and perfect will"* (Romans 12:2). Success comes from thinking right and the role of every leader is to create a way of thinking that lines up with everything that the heart believes.

9. Second day

On the first day God created light. With no celestial assistance light radiated from heaven. That light is the light of revelation. On the second day God created sky. Sky represents the vast array of opportunity that's available to those who bring their imagination under subjection to their revelation. Our imagination is one of our greatest heavenly gifts. The best of Christianity never takes place when we submit our finances or our time to Christ. Neither does it take place when we give all of our talent or all of our energy to Christ. The best is reserved for the creativity locked up in our imaginings. The greatest of our sinning comes through an un-submitted imagination. Conversely, the greatest works of grace and power have happened when our revelation has united with our imagination. The sky becomes the limit. Leadership learns to capture people's imagination to create the greatest gains for the Kingdom.

10. Second stage

"Come up here..." (Revelation 4:1). There are new levels to attain and new stages to conquer. Success is broken down into modules. Between each level is a series of steps that, when completed, lead to a whole new level of operation and success. It may be time for the second stage of success. A success culture always moves from a current personal best to a better personal best. It spirals up, not down. Most of a leader's life is spent planning for the next big thing. Beware of settling. The pioneer

spirit wasn't dished out to just a few frontier men. It was given to everyone.

Essential leadership kit
(for getting started on the journey)

- Maximise the power of vision through always creating a possibility culture and developing the language of hope.
- Don't "over-promise". Lead the people by always operating between the realms of reality and possibility.
- Redefine success outside of the narrowness of simply "winning".
- Starting right is essential. If you get the right direction and start to create momentum you're already on the journey of success.

The Diary Archives

After being prompted by the Hillsborough disaster, when one hundred people died in a football stadium in Sheffield, my wife and I took the plunge to leave Australia and pioneer a church in the UK that would hopefully become a nationally impacting church. Hope City Church began as, "The Hope of Sheffield Christian Church" in 1991. After seeing a lot of growth in the first five years, a conflict arose that saw a third of the people leave. This diary begins two years after that crisis.

2nd March 1998
On the 19th September, 1993, Dave Cartledge, a national leader of the Australian Assemblies of God, prophesied that our church would go through the gates of iron and brass of our city that many had confronted before but had never overcome. He also declared that we would go in the front way and not the back and the

outcome of this would be known across the land. He declared that the Lord had many people in the city and was determined to do a great work. He also declared that there were many adversaries both outside the church and within it who would rise up and try to prevent the work that God wanted to do.

This diary begins one and a half years after the beginning of the unfolding of this prophecy with over one third of our congregation deciding to leave the church within the space of a single month. The battle lines of division had been drawn. I had confronted what I believed to be a spirit of self-importance, light footedness and a spirit of control that had slowly developed over our first five years amongst some key leaders and the outcome of this confrontation was far more severe than I could have imagined. These leaders felt exactly the same way about me! Numerically our church hit the ceiling at 270 people and would go no further unless serious issues were addressed. Our mindset, now, was to run as fast as we could into our future destiny and leave our past way behind us.

I had found a new confidence in God that gave me the strength to do what had to be done. My previous lack of confidence had led to many key decisions being deferred to others and had created a power vacuum that was being filled by certain leaders who had stopped growing in their Christian walk. They needed to change or step down.

Yesterday in church, Jenny (my wife) prophesied that we were now going through the promised gates and starting to enter our inheritance. There was no applause and no electricity in the air. The numbers were at their lowest in a long time and no one got saved. I preached on, "God gives grace to the humble" and declared that that's what I want to be. I had recently spoken to a group of churches in Lancashire and felt really bad that I had embellished the ministry write-up of myself (including the huge measurements of our "just signed for" Megacentre building) simply to impress. I vowed never to do that again.

It was strange for my wife to prophesy such a dramatic event in the midst of such an un-dramatic service. We usually reserved great prophecies for the electric times, of which we had had many, but this was to be very different. It's been a tough road not having seen any numerical increase in years and, in actual fact, witnessing a severe decrease. Deep down though there is a confidence – an assurance that our loss of people is to be seen more in the light of the reduction of Gideon's army than a retraction of the hand of God. We have great faith for the future. In the spirit of faith I have chosen to journal a history of events leading up to what I hope to see: a "Sheffield Revival". If it's true that we have gone through unseen gates to the city that have thwarted many in the past, then this must be the beginning of the next significant move of the Holy Spirit.

It's only recently that I have learned again not to despise the day of small beginnings. Two recent testimonies have really encouraged me: a woman called Louise gave up her engagement because of the call of God upon her life and her commitment to our church (her fiancé requested that she relocate.) Secondly, a guy called Colin gave up a large wage increase that was offered to him if he would relocate to Leeds, also because of his commitment to the destiny of our church. Within weeks, both of these people have seen souls saved as their reward.

In last night's church service we had three commitments to Christ. One was Steve, a manager from Pizza Hut (who was saved through Louise), and another was a lady who runs a cat sanctuary.

An amazing thing happened today. We got a letter from a couple who were major players in the first five years in the life of our church, but had turned sharply on us and sowed vast quantities of seeds of malice and unrest. They had been hugely instrumental in the big clearout of the summer of 1996. It was a battering time of intense persecution and hardship, just as Dave

Cartledge had prophesied back in 1993. (Only one person in the whole congregation linked what had happened with the prophecy.) Today they extended grace towards us to forgive us of our debt. Also, the wife of another former leader (who had also left with a bang and taken many with him) rang up my wife and asked for a time of reconciliation. We found it amazing that these two things happened today. I sent a card to the first couple and told the Lord that I'd be open to allowing them back into our lives and restoring relationship. It's a scary thought and I feel quite vulnerable, but I realise that God expects more from me than from others.

5th March 1998

My old senior minister in Australia, Chris Peterson, used to frequently repeat the phrase, "Don't watch the waves, watch the tide." It's a lesson that I often fail in. Last night Jenny and I were gutted by the absence of two new Christians at our midweek meeting. A few years ago I was running past a house near where we lived and I felt God tell me that great things would happen in that house. I regularly heard piano playing coming from it and recently decided to initiate things by asking if my son, who is six years of age, could have lessons. After a short time the couple had given their hearts to the Lord. We have been really banking on them being a part of the new life-blood and new move of the Spirit in our church. Something's not right. We feel like they've become our friends and yet our lifestyle is so intense it's really hard for us to maintain a close friendship outside of leadership. It's also hard for others to understand that. They've definitely pulled back and we're really disappointed. It's made me aware that behind a lot of my anger and cynicism lays deep veins of this kind of disappointment. Jen shared her grief and disappointment with Sophia and she told Jen it was time to let go and release them from the underlying pressure of our high expectations. We're starting to feel better. I've also been encouraged today from the book of Zephaniah that records that God is the one who "restores fortune" and He's the one who is "exalting over me in happy song". God is about to do great things.

6th March 1998

This has been such a difficult week. In checking our Sunday School register I've noted that so many young families have abandoned the cause of late and made their final decision to leave the church. An older man came to me yesterday and said he was also leaving with his wife. I usually let go easily in the knowledge that the horse has already bolted, but I fought for him in conversation in a last ditch effort to get him to see the truth about his life and his future. It now seems like time wasted. I heard yesterday that one of our ex-musicians, who was taken off our music team because of immorality, was now on the warpath against me claiming, amongst other things, that I was truly a manipulator (the devil knows I can't stand that!).

Today's update:

Our leadership conflict that led to our church conflict was brought to the surface and exacerbated by the inclusion of two new senior leaders onto our leadership team. Because of my affiliation with them and a change in the decision making centre of gravity amongst the leadership, a change in leadership dynamic developed that had to be resolved and overcome.

Louise has become one of our awesome Congregational Pastors and Colin is our Church Business Manager. Both have become great friends. Steve is a fantastic Building Manager and his wife Siobhan has become our Executive Pastor.

Note

1. Benjamin Zander, *The Art of Possibility*, Penguin, 2002.

There is No Such Thing As a Leap of Faith

The Confusion of the Faith Life

Because leadership is about making the journey from today's world into tomorrow's world, it is essential that we teach people how to succeed along the journey. Leadership specialises in marathons, not sprints. Quick bursts of energy and adrenalin are an essential part of successful leadership, but having people come the whole distance and not set up camp on the wrong side of the Jordan is vital.

In this chapter we're going to look at the real journey of faith and how it differs greatly from what most people think is normal. We're also going to expose the myth of the "leap" of faith and encourage you to create a leadership that deals in the power of steps, not jumps.

The real journey of leadership

It's rare to find a really good movie. Just about every time we go to the movies we expect it to be as good as they say it is. That's rarely the case! It's rare that you wear half of the clothes that you packed to take on holiday, yet every time you go away, you pack twice as much as you need. It's rare to find fairy-tale endings for people who live without God, yet, we hope that it's not the case.

Leadership is about teaching people what to expect and what not to expect. I've found nine things that we expect to be common in ministry, but are actually very, very rare!

1. It's rare to have everything go according to plan

"Bad-a-bing, bad-a-boom" is a recent addition to the Oxford portfolio, meaning that everything falls effortlessly and seamlessly into place. We often look at other churches and ministers and think that they always seem to land on their feet. They look like they're always having a "bad-a-boom" moment. Well, I'm a believer in things looking good, but I also know that it's rare for anyone to land on their feet (like in Olympic gymnastics) without a wobble. It's rare that churches simply grow and expand, moving from one summer season to the next. It's far more common that winters precede summers. Why do so few things go according to plan? Why don't we have more instant and consistent success? Why is there always something not right? Answer – our greatest dangers lie not in a lack confidence, but in over-confidence.

More people die coming down Everest than climbing it. It's what successful athletes protect themselves against when they prepare mentally before every race. Their greatest danger is being blasé through over-confidence and losing the prize they so long to gain. God often reminds us of our frailty. Even at the best of times, there are things that nag us. They are there to remind us that it's not by might or by power, but definitely by His Spirit!. Even when we finally accomplish great exploits, we find one of God's "post-it notes" stuck somewhere, reminding us that *all* the glory goes to Him. Stop blaming the devil when there's a hiccup. Thank God that He's saving you from yourself. It's usually not the sand in the dune that slows someone down from achieving great things, but the sand in the eye. God is making sure that our eyes are constantly upon Him from beginning to end.

2. It's rare to have all of your achievements standing before you all at once

Wouldn't we all love to have the thousands of people we've helped in our lifetime standing in front of us each and every Sunday (representing all our blood, sweat and blessings). It's a rare thing, however, to have all our achievements in one room all at one time. Even if you are able to congregate much of what you do, your greatest influence is happening outside of your vision, rather than directly within it.

For a start, we live a faith life, which means that most of what we do is related to future, unseen accomplishments, rather than presently attained goals. But it's encouraging to know that our influence can extend beyond what we see in front of us. When Paul was speaking to King Agrippa in Acts 26, he said *"I pray God that not only you but all who are listening to me today may become what I am, except for these chains"* (v. 29). He saw his words going "over the wall", reaching not only the king, but everyone who worked for him. Our influence is the same – going way over the wall of who is simply present in one single meeting.

In British politics it was the death of a leader called John Smith that made the way for Tony Blair. His rise to being Prime Minister was the result of an unintentional event. A lot of what we do unintentionally can become the key to our future intentions. Your influence goes far beyond what you could ever imagine. You have no idea how your careless words impact, just as your carefully selected words do. When I go to conferences it's often what the speaker says outside of his notes that makes a greater impression on me than what he intentionally planned to say. It's vital for leadership to heap a faith perspective on everything we're involved in and know that our influence is much larger than we see on a Sunday!

3. It's rare to find that what you're doing really suits you

Sometimes, when I'm out shopping with my wife, she picks up a dress and says, "I love it . . . it's really me." It's a rare moment, but when she says it, I know exactly what she means. Through a lot of "gifting appraisal" programmes we have tried to create churches where people end up saying the same thing as my wife: "I love it . . . it's really me." I've realised, however, that it's a rare thing that you do stuff that really suits you, particularly during the pioneer stages of ministry. If it's true that my function in the body of Christ is to always be using my primary gifts, why do I spend so much time not using them? I've concluded that the foundation of all I do isn't only gifting, it's getting the job that needs to be done – done!

Making people too conscious of their gifts without blasting home the purpose of the gifts will always result in an overdose of self-indulgence. In the past we've had to cut down a lot of "moving in the gifts" because its focus was more toward the giver than the recipient. The gift was dirtied by the motivation that propelled it. Tell someone they can't prophesy and they can't pray at a particular time and test their reaction. It will always expose hidden motives. I have found that the soap that keeps my gifts clean and sparkling is the sublime acts of service that I do outside of my primary gifting. Colin Dye of Kensington Temple once said that after taking people through a "what's your gift" programme he would then make them do the opposite of their gift inclination. Welcome to the Bible College of life!

4. It's rare that God gives directional prophecy

We live in a world that's itching to know the future. Horoscopes and mediums abound. It's the same with churches. There is a big demand to know what the future holds and huge pressure upon ministers to speculate about future outcomes. I've learnt that God only reveals a small number of things, keeping many things hidden for a future time. Psalm 97 says that, *"Clouds and thick darkness surround Him"* (v. 2). Even with the headlights of revelation on full beam, darkness still surrounds our peripheral vision. We will only ever know in part. This is not an excuse – it's an encouragement! As I've already said in chapter 1, when God says, "I know the plans I have for you," He's actually saying that because He knows the plans, you don't have to. It's God's business to know the plans, not yours. To know God's nature has a far greater benefit than knowing God's plans. That's why the Bible is a revelation of God Himself, rather than a route map of your personal future. To put our faith in the nature of God is to trust God through "thick clouds and darkness".

Recently a voluntary staff member of mine said that he wouldn't be staying with us on the journey unless he understood why we were making some of the decisions that we were making. It came down not to an issue of understanding, but an issue of trust. Would he trust us with the future, or would he wait until he could see it for himself? Your people don't need a futuristic word from God but a "naturistic" word from God! A prophecy is primarily meant for edification, exhortation and comfort (1 Corinthians 14:3). Let it be so. It is important that we teach people to drive in the headlights of their revelation and not wait until they know what's around the next corner before they start moving. Progressive revelation only begins when we're faithful to the first word that God gives without waiting for a second one.

5. It's rare to fly as the crow flies
Why has it taken so long to see my church established and growing? Why does God move so slowly? Why does He rarely

use short cuts? Between revelation and realisation is a long and winding road, but character formation is all part of our real destination. God's will isn't just to build church building extensions and to see hundreds of people swept into the kingdom. His goal is also to make us more like Him in order to prepare us to accommodate all that He's about to do. That takes patience. Patience always requires the winding road. The testing of our faith produces character that's essential for when we are finally handed the keys to our new church building. "Don't think it strange" is a scripture for those of us who do find it strange when things go into reverse just as we're almost able to touch our destination. When you've acted in good faith and you've excelled in your quest to give glory to God, your future now rests in His providence. Short cut or long cut, God will never break faith. He will accomplish that for which He called you forth.

I recently painted a picture using water colours which ended up one big mess. When I turned the picture over in order to start again on a new work of art, I saw that the spillage had seeped through and been absorbed by the underside of the paper. It looked so great that I framed the underside. What God is creating behind the scenes is pretty impressive. He's working a beautiful design that far outweighs all we can see in front of us. The depth of colour and spontaneous beauty of your unplanned life (and goals) can have more impact than your deliberate architecture of life. Jesus did as many miracles on the way to His destination as He did at the destinations themselves. Teach the people you lead that everything is working to their advantage. Their "spillage" is leaving a powerful imprint in the world around them – much more than they will ever realise.

6. It's rare to find the perfect church

Everyone thinks that out in the blue yonder (or on the God channel!) lies the perfect church – one where all of your gifts are valued and used; one where you meet friends with similar interests as you, and one where there's a great sense of belonging. If you ever get all three at the same time, it's an exception. The perfect church is always the imperfect church. Let me explain! It's perfect to have some hypocrite sitting next to you just to expose and expel your judgemental spirit. It's perfect to have people who ignore us so our value comes from God. It's perfect to have seasons where there's little sense of the presence of God in our services, otherwise we may just be switching from living by faith to living by feelings. The perfect church is one that continues to provoke people to being expanded into Christ's likeness. God must prepare the vessel. Perfection, therefore, is closer than you think.

The church I was the full-time Youth Pastor in was one that basked in country music. I hate country music. For God, though, it was perfect. I had to put aside my leanings toward rock music and soak my life and ministry with country music. To surrender personal preference for corporate unity is essential in building a powerful church. It's funny to see how so many people's personal preferences have dictated everything in church buildings, from the covering of the communion table to the flower arrangements. For new ministers, removing such items can cause World War III, because of the domination of individual preference. This is a sign of a weak church.

Never think that the perfect church is the mega church on television or the one they're leaving your church to be a part of. Iron has always sharpened iron and God makes sure that every church is weighted with stuff that annoys, ignores and dissatisfies. It's the Holy Spirit's job to rub you up the wrong way, reveal the real you, and then prepare you to meet the real Jesus.

7. It's rare to find the perfect partner

It's rare to find total compatibility! When you look at others, you often think that they're a couple made in heaven! That's only ever partly true. Compatibility is a strange thing. If you married someone who has everything you put on your dream list, you may find yourself in a really incompatible situation! When God puts couples together, He often draws together people who are a little different from each other. The reason behind it is that you need it. Imagine someone just like you! You need someone who'll complement all that you are; someone who'll be strong in the areas where you are weak and vice versa.

The world sees compatibility as two people who listen to Frank Sinatra and go line dancing, yet real relationships are not built on external togetherness, they are built on a true understanding of the rhythm of the soul, as well as a uniting of strengths and love to become one in spirit. A great key for love and happiness has always been "bendability". It's the ability to occasionally surrender your rights without losing your personality. Stop aiming for compatibility and start building a church on the real stuff that great relationships are actually made of: love ... actually!

8. It's rare that lightning ever strikes twice

We fear that if something has happened before it might well happen again. The truth is that 99% of all fears rarely become a reality. Isaiah 43 tells us to "fear not" because God is with us. "Though we go through the waters, we will not drown, and though we go through the fires we will not burn" (see verse 2). Our God has gone before us and has cleared the way for a life of faith and future success. *"Fear not, for I have redeemed you"* (v. 1). If Jesus went to the cross to redeem you from the quarry of sin and powerlessness, He's not about to let you go from the grasp of His hand. "You are mine," He says. "You were bought with a great price." Lightning will not strike again.

It's also true that if you've grown and matured through the difficulties of the past, it's rare that you'll ever need to be fully subject to them again. If you've gained your heavenly Father's love out of your earthly father's rejection, and if you've trusted in God after having your trust broken by your closest friend, it's rare that God will take you around the same mountain. It's onwards and upwards for the child of God.

It's also rare that moments of brilliance ever strike twice in someone's life. You can't have a second honeymoon. You can't manufacture "magic moments". When Peter was on the mountain where Jesus was transfigured into heavenly glory, he wanted to freeze frame it and keep it going forever. It was not to be. In life God is committed to giving you "moments of brilliance" – amazing moments that build lasting memories. Stop allowing people to hang on to former memories and ask God to help them to forget the former things and look to the "new things" that He is waiting to do for them.

9. It's rare that time doesn't fly

They say time flies when you're having fun. The truth is time does nothing but fly. Because of that you need to ensure you've got your direction right! The rudder is a tiny part of a great ship, yet one of the most important elements. If your motivations are pure, your intentions are in line with your convictions, and you don't allow yourself to be distracted, you'll do well. Hebrews tells us to "... *pay more careful attention, therefore, to what we have heard, so that we do not drift away*" (Hebrews 2:1). Drifting is the malaise of many. Be true to your vision and true to your belief. Bring everything into line.

Leadership is all about lifting and lowering expectations. People looking for "overnight success" are often paralysed by their expectations. On the other hand, people whose service for God has become slavery to God often miss the blessings and harvests that God has for them, simply through reduced expectations. It's time for leadership to lead the way along the journey of destiny God has set before us.

It's all about the power of a step

In all of the journeys of faith that were traversed by the heroes of the Bible, not one was ever involved in a "leap of faith". Most people think that there lies a huge chasm between them and their future that can only be accomplished by a gigantic leap. The truth is, what lies in front of them is a journey that requires only a simple step. Steps belong to man; leaps belong to God.

It has often been said that Joseph hung on to his dreams throughout the whole length of his thirteen year ordeal at the hands of injustice. Where does it say that in the Bible? When Joseph finally met up with his brothers after being parted for over twenty years, the Bible recalls, *"Then he remembered his dreams about them . . . "* (Genesis 42:9) There's an inference here – the dreams were not in the forefront of his thinking all of the time. The story of Joseph is not a story about his ability to hold on to dreams. It's not a story about the ability to exercise giant leaps of faith. The story of Joseph is a story of steps. There are a number of steps in Joseph's journey to breakthrough.

- *Step 1* – Joseph did well for Potiphar
- *Step 2* – Joseph did well for the jailer
- *Step 3* – Joseph did great for the butler and baker
- *Step 4* – Joseph did superbly well for Pharaoh
- *Step 5* – There isn't one!

Four small steps for Joseph; one giant leap for the kingdom of God. Steps belong to us, but success belongs to God.

The Bible is a book of small steps that lead to a culmination of giant leaps. Again, there is no such thing in the Bible as a leap of faith. Psalm 37:23 in the New King James version says, *"The steps of a good man are ordered by the LORD"* It's talking about steps – not leaps, pirouettes or riverdancing. Just steps; simple, clear steps. For every person who is in your church, the next step for them is simple, attainable and straightforward. God never requires us to do the impossible. That realm belongs to Him.

While I'm on this train of thought, there's no such thing as a "great man of God"! Only a "man of a great God"! When we refer to some people as "great" we think they got there by leaping over canyons and floating above the storms. They actually got there by the same means as you – the power of a step. There is also no such thing as a "great prayer". Prayer is no magic formula. It is simply another step in the right direction. It's always one small step for man, one giant leap for the kingdom of God. We step, God leaps. Here are the four most common diseases of dynamic dreamers who are caught up in the whole palaver of "leaps of faith".

1. They never earth their dream

They become like New Age travellers, never staying long enough for their dreams to take root. So many people want to visit London, but within days of arriving, they're off to Paris! They've got the "All I got was this lousy t-shirt" t-shirt, but they never really explored London. Dreamers, at some stage, need to stop dreaming and start "earthing" their dream.

2. They're paralysed by their dream

Without the knowledge of the power of the step, the acute awareness of the gulf between current reality and future desire can bring a sense of powerlessness. People replace stepping with talking. Their talking is simply an escape route from the daily life of faith. Powerlessness is not a bad thing. We can't perform a miracle even if we try. We can't save the lost, heal the sick, or build the Church. What we can do is step out and expect a collision with the mighty power of Heaven.

3. They fail to seed their dream

God created man out of something He'd already created – dust. On days one to five of creation He declared, "Let there be ..." On day six He took the seed out of what He'd already created and declared man into existence. What are you doing with the dust under your feet? With a sling, David slew Goliath. The seed to every miracle is within your grasp. The water pots are here. The little boy's lunch is close. The key to your church's growth lies not in the realm of the miraculous, but within the dust of the people who already surround you. With dust, God creates diamonds.

4. They grow impatient with the dream

Joseph's success came because he successfully navigated each of the steps to success. Each step looked like a backward step, yet each one was actually a step closer to breakthrough. Often our first step runs counter-culture to the promises we have been given. God promises prosperity – we step into famine. Often our last step is a step of sheer trust, not in any dream, but purely in the One from whom dreams come. The darkest point is just before the dawn. The answer is to keep making tracks and establish momentum.

It's time to believe the sky's the limit – then ignore it. It's time for a step of faith. In the middle of a storm a man said to his friend in the boat, "Shall we pray or shall we row?" His friend replied, "Let's pray *and* row." Prayer is a step. Rowing is a step. One is step one, the other is step two. Never underestimate the power of a step.

Essential leadership kit (for the journey of faith)

- The journey may be long, but remember that God is preparing you for future greatness.
- Never compare your fruit with someone else's. Your influence goes far beyond the borders of what you can see today.
- Teach your people to stop looking for directional prophecy and to begin to step out in the words that they have already received.
- If we do what we can do, we allow God to do what only He can do. Steps belong to man, success belongs to God.

The Diary Archives

16th March 1998

It's been a good week. We had a great article in the *Star* – the city's newspaper. It said, "Thank goodness for Dave Gilpin and his congregation!" Well, that's the favour of God. It was all about our dream for our new facilities called, "The Megacentre". The article could well have been along the lines of "cult moves into new premises". It sure feels like a new day. I'm still really inspired by *The Purpose Driven Church* and about the whole movement of a church from the crowd to the core. I feel a fresh restructuring coming on for later in the year which I will present to my two assistants over the coming weeks.

I am still really disappointed by people who just can't get into the life of the church and who continue to isolate themselves in hard times. Thank God for Steve – the whole of Pizza Hut know about his conversion and everyone holds a lot of respect for him. I'm sure that God has a great call upon his life. I've already got plans!

I preached on "The Appointed Time" from the book of Habakkuk yesterday. I humorously declared the well-worn spiel that the safest aeroplane to be on was the one that I was on because of my "unfulfilled prophecy", which reflected a new found confidence in my God-given future. I used the analogy that, "the Mercedes is already in the garage" – in other words, the great plans of God are already in the bag. You can miss it but you can't invent it. A collision with destiny is drawing closer every second, all culminating at God's appointed time. I declared that inside I was sleeping in the knowledge that everything was signed, sealed and delivered, but on the outside I was busy doing good to all. It was a great sermon – now all I need do is to live it. Thank you Lord for all of your plans. Help me not to lose faith over what I see today. Help me to love You even though there be "no fruit on the vine". I will praise You and trust You forever because You are the Father of heaven!

30th March 1998

I preached at youth on Friday night and had a fresh revelation of an old thought: we're not here to build a big church, but to change a big city and a big world. A big church is too small a vision.

On Sunday the church cheered when we heard live over the telephone that a group from our church had reached the Hungarian/Romanian border on their way to ministering in Central Europe. They'd seen 40 decisions for Christ in the past week. We're all a part of it. Also on Sunday, a couple from New Zealand started a new church in Doncaster – a town of 100,000 people. They had 65 people come to their first service. We're also a part of that! A couple from Kiev in the Ukraine called up today to say that each Sunday 20 people were making decisions for Christ. They said that over 550 people were attending their home groups. We're a part of that as well! It's a fresh revelation!

My Sunday message was on the "river" from Ezekiel, focusing on the place where your feet no longer touch the ground. You're out of control – He's in control. It's the place I'm in. We've done a lot of prayer and fasting and made a lot of plans. It just seems to be the season for praise and thanksgiving and spending time in the river – all else seems to be striving. We're waiting for the Lord!

Last weekend I ministered in Northern Ireland. I feel a real bond with the place. I even got a call from a young pastor in Londonderry when I got back, looking for help. (I almost didn't go on this trip and nearly missed out on this great opportunity.)

11th April 1998

Tomorrow is Easter Sunday and marks the end of the 7th year of the church. I don't think anyone realises it as there is no one currently attending the church from the first Easter Sunday (except for Jenny!). It's a funny feeling. I feel a little like the woman who broke open the jar of expensive perfume and poured it over Jesus' feet. I feel like so much of what we've done has purely been worship unto Jesus costing some of the best years of my life. I can see how we've faithfully taken the baton of God and held it strong on behalf of the core of the church and all who are a part of the next generation. I can see that God has created in us deep wells from heaven that have been produced through trial and endurance. Much of all that has happened has been foundational and underground. I have measured success externally for far too long. Our eyes are now off numerics and onto the deep work that God's done in our hearts. It still really pains us to see people that we've invested so much time into not rise up to the challenge and not enter into the new victories that God had in store for them.

Glyn has just left on a train to Manchester on his way to Kiev, discouraged at the results he's been getting in the youth ministry after so much work. I really feel for him. I know that God's deepening him and I figure that it takes greater faith for someone to keep going when they don't see a breakthrough than it does for someone who sees an earlier breakthrough. Glyn could go to Kiev with confidence that he was a man of faith and had something to say even in a "revival" situation. I shared that with him and it seemed to make a difference.

I read today that a committee for the European parliament who are looking into rising cults in Europe have decided to place all denominations not recognised by the World Council of Churches in the cult category. We are now alongside the Church of Scientology!

We're now in such a needy situation regarding the new building for our church. We need thousands of pounds to move into the middle section of the Megacentre alone. We're way overspent in our main account. We've tried everything to balance the books and minimise expenditure. If we use up money coming in August for our training school we'll have none to help offset our impending increased loan repayments for the basic shell of the Megacentre. We're in the zone I preach on often – deep water! All of our exit doors are closed and we need a miracle. We have so little time and many people we've asked to help us financially are unable to assist us until a much later date (or so they say). We really don't want to be foolish by getting work done in the Megacentre that we can't pay for now and yet we don't want the project placed on hold and lose the momentum we have. We are desperate for God to move. People often say faith is spelt R.I.S.K. and I know why. There is an underlying certainty that it will all come to pass, yet much of the visual looks daunting and overwhelming. The risk is that you risk everything for the certainty that God is faithful. I took the scripture, "believe that you have received it and it shall be yours" to heart the other day and I really believe that God will break through. All the waiting!

I so want to be an inspirational leader and I so want to see the people's faith rewarded. A week ago we received thousands of pounds worth of good quality office furniture for the centre courtesy of cast-offs from Leeds City Council. That was a great start.

16th April 1998

We've just returned from a four day break in Blackpool. I love holidays. God supplied our needs right down to the last pound and I was able to buy some new shoes and a new top. God has been good to us. Usually when I come back from breaks I begin to panic about the state of the church and what's happened while I've been away. Today was no exception. The financial constraints that were now upon us hit me hard and the possibility of putting one of our full-time workers on part time, as well as cutting the wages of all the staff, was now a serious possibility. I really need to take it to God. Without a major breakthrough there will be major changes. Tonight I asked God to speak afresh to cast new light and faith on our situation. We need miracles all round. I need to make some major decisions.

I told Glyn that we needed a financial breakthrough and he suggested that we got all the church to fast and pray. I told him that I felt that we'd done all that we could and it was now in God's hands. I really believe that the people now need to see some miracles for all the sacrifices that they'd made.

It's so hard getting a balance between faith and what looks like sound financial management. Faith never looks logical or naturally attainable. We are now in a crucial period with only ten weeks to come up with huge amounts of money.

5th May 1998

The company that were to take the lease off us for our existing church building has pulled out. We've leased the warehouse for three years and have one year to go. We are now paying hefty amounts towards the mortgage repayments on our Megacentre facility. We're about to move into our first stage of renovations of our new centre and the company pulling out on the lease is certainly a setback. At times life feels like one of those computer screensavers that have mountains that don't gradually grow from the horizon but suddenly come into view from the left side of the screen. Faith remains the land in which we live and breathe. There's no other way we can do this!

15th May 1998

Today I received news that another large charity would not be supporting us financially in our new venture. I had a prophecy from some guy who saw a large cheque book open up for me with the scripture, "Ask and ye shall receive." After he shared it I began to cry as I caught the revelation that God has seen our endurance and hard work. Because this guy knew nothing of our situation it was a real sign that God was with us.

I've always found it hard to correct leaders around me and at the same time be encouraging to them. I also find it especially difficult with older men. I never had older men around me while growing up and my relationship with my dad was always quite distant. I feel great today, though, because I was able to correct an older member of my team about his wrong attitudes and at the same time create a closer bond with him. God has definitely granted me a new ability!

30th June 1998

It's been a month now since we moved into the Megacentre. I felt challenged to sow our first Sunday's offering directly to our new local community. I ran it past my oversight because it would mean that we would be giving away next week's wages. They all agreed! The offering came to one of the largest we'd ever had . . .

and we were giving it away! A week later we had our opening night and the previous owner of the building, who is one of the directors of Sheffield United, was present with his wife. Our last encounter had been a difficult one, firstly because of recent complications with the payment of VAT and secondly because we brought him down from a potential ten year lease on the building of £1.4 million, to purchasing the entire property for £200,000. I was surprised to see him at the opening. Everyone knew who he was and the night must have made a big impression on him. He came into my office at the end of the service, got his cheque book out, and wrote a cheque for £1,000. That was both a miracle and a return of around half of the money that we had just sown into our local community.

We're still paying rent on our old building as well as paying the mortgage on our new building. It continues to be a stretching time. We have made a decision, however, not to reduce any of the staff wages this coming September, but to actually increase them. It can only be accomplished by supernatural intervention. We have also decided to use £20,000 that we had designated for heating and spend it on the first stage of our indoor children's centre. We still have three months until the cold weather is upon us and so we've taken a decision to believe for the money for the heating equipment before the weather turns.

The whole team has worked so well in this time of great pressure. I'm amazed at the unity, the faith, and the respect that's emerged over the last few months. Personally, I'm not used to such great respect and authority. For years, whenever I corrected someone, mayhem and fall out would always result. We're in the midst of incredible change which includes our location, our church structure, and even our style of service, yet everyone is working so well. I think change has become part of our value system rather than a thorn in our side.

Today, I'm flying to Australia with a minister from one of Sheffield's more established churches to attend the Hillsong Conference. It feels odd leaving the church for two weeks at a crucial time, but I think it may be God's plan to de-stress me. I get obsessively focused! I've got to allow the "seeds of faith" to grow without getting hung up on the "brown dirt" I see every day. Also, I've got to allow others in leadership to take the reigns on many of the things that I've initiated.

Two Sundays ago I was wearing one of the two suits that I own. I remember consciously thinking to myself how much I loved the suit I was in (and how great it looked on me), and immediately felt the Holy Spirit encourage me to give it away to Glyn. That happened at the end of the Sunday morning meeting. At the same time, Glyn and Sophia had felt impressed to give away the money that they'd saved for a suit and place it in the Sunday morning offering. (They had a serious argument after the service because they'd agreed to give away half the money and yet Sophia gave away all of the money!) At night I came up to Glyn and asked him if he'd like my suit and promptly handed it to him. It was a great moment. It was one of those great miraculous moments that I'll remember for a long time. Jenny and I also emptied our bank account and gave all we had away. We really believe that God wants to increase us financially so we can both enjoy some special things and become bigger channels of blessing to others. I really want to bless Jenny for all her sacrifice by building a deck off the back of our house, so she can lie out in the sun (which she almost worships) in solitude and comfort. She loves the sun and getting as much of it as possible has been an art form for her while living in England. It's been funny coming from a sunny nation, to find every second car in the UK with a sun roof. I can understand it now. Life in England has always been easier for me than Jenny, not only because I don't miss the hot weather, but also because of her almost overwhelming sense of isolation that's not been helped by her mum being 10,000 miles away.

Today's update:
Glyn and Sophia have had two children and continue to flow with zeal and enthusiasm as Associate Ministers of Hope City Church, as well as spearheading Audacious Youth Ministries and Youth Alive UK.

25th August 1998
Last night I had a terrible sleep. My body was exhausted, yet my adrenalin was pumping late into the night. I feel disorientated today and really tired. I've decided to work from home. We started our children's centre (stage 1) two days ago and I think that it's affected me. I don't think that it's the immediate pressure that's pushed me over, but an accumulation of pressure that's making me lose energy really quickly. It's a bit like a soldier who's been on the front line for too long. A holiday is in order.

Yesterday we depleted all our church bank account and borrowed some money internally in a personal arrangement with a congregation member. Between late yesterday and this morning we got news of around £8,000 being sent to us from various trusts. We have also had a miracle with a heating system! We have taken up the offer of a second-hand one that could possibly do our entire building for a really knockdown price! It's currently in another building and we've managed to get all the radiators out and now need some demolition work to get the two massive boilers out. There's only five weeks until the cold sets in. We still need a lot of money (on top of the personal loan) to get the heating system all set up.

I don't think a day goes past without some kind of dramatic news. It's as if we are in a prolonged transition time that never seems to settle back to some kind of normality. Maybe this is the new "normal".

I'm concerned with myself because I get little adrenalin attacks that then get a little worse when I think that they might be little panic attacks. I've had some spells when I've just felt distant – strangely distant. I've stayed home today just to avoid any undue pressure. Because of the way I'm wired, I use up a lot of energy just talking to people and need a lot of space in between appointments (which I just don't get). I easily get uptight about such small things. Yesterday, I was almost possessed by the background music we put on in the entrance foyer of the Megacentre. I've got a fetish for background music and get so consumed about it being at the right level to create a bright and buoyant atmosphere. I've got to pull back from details and get some relief! Glyn just called and said that I need an outside interest! It's true – I'd love to go and see the Bee Gees at Wembley Stadium next Saturday night. If I don't get some miracle tickets real soon, I'm going to order some at the box office!

3rd September 1998

I spent a lot of time over the weekend crying out for a breakthrough. I had a long time of worship and really prayed for a recovery emotionally, physically and spiritually. Now, four days on, I'm amazed. I feel great. The stress has gone and I went to a prayer meeting and felt really lifted. That's a story in itself, because for at least nine months I have felt a bit repelled by prayer meetings. I think I've felt exhausted praying for things that I have prayed for hundreds of times before. I was amazed at how refreshing it was to again be interceding for the kingdom of God outside of my own personal times with God. I know God has done a miracle in me. I'm committed to a new lifestyle of exercise, devotions and getting into church later to help me stay sane. I think it's working – I feel fresher and friendlier!

We opened our Megakids and Megabites fun centre almost two weeks ago and it's starting to be a real winner. It gives me great satisfaction to see the church rising up in such a way that it both blesses the local community and equips the saints. We've organised the church programme and vision into five zones that help lead people along what we've called the "journey of discovery". Somebody becomes a part of our community zone activities, then moves into discovery zone activities, gets saved, and moves into our foundation zone, and then into the programmes of the growth and equippers zone. I love the concept. The community centre should only be the tip of the iceberg of what's really going on in the life of the church. I'm also excited because the vision unites the community centre with everything else the church does, so you don't get left with "community centre" versus "the church". It's all "church" – the church in action. For the first time in the history of the church (seven years) I can stand back and get a real sense of satisfaction that we've got our direction right and we've got a brilliant team (out of 250 people, 23 are working either part time, full time, voluntary or on an internship) and we've got that indispensable and generally un-preached about quality called "momentum" beginning to rise up, creating within us an unstoppable feeling.

4th September 1998

Somebody has shouted me a ticket to see the Bee Gees at Wembley Stadium tomorrow night. God is good.

First Become a One Man Band

The Confusion of Team

The headlining band on the penultimate night of Britain's most infamous rock festival, Glastonbury, wasn't what you'd class a "regular" band. One young lad on electric guitar and one lary young woman on drums. How on earth did "The White Stripes" ever rise to the top of international success? They don't even have a bass guitarist! Every band needs a bass player. "Not so," says the new generation. But it wasn't the fans that said "not so" first – it was The White Stripes themselves. It was they who determined that what will be, will be. They may not have a bass guitarist, but what they have got, as well as great music, is what we all absolutely need to achieve our God given destiny – audacious confidence.

Through a lack of confidence many "bass players" are added to leadership teams which would have been better off without them. Church splits are often down to a leadership split. The problem, though, is not the split. The problem was sown way back when the team was established. The driving force behind the creation of the team was not purely creating "better music" – it was driven by a feeling of inadequacy. The feeling that, without a "bass player", we would have an incomplete sound to our ministry.

Before anyone creates a successful team they have to firstly come into a measure of personal success. In this chapter we're going to be looking at the need for you to become personally successful before you can create a great team. We're going to look at the four stages of team development that must take place before a "dream team" is established, how to use your team to release vision to the people, and what a team member goes through in order to become a great team member!

1. Power of one

Your confidence will determine the outcome of your entire life. It's not what you believe that counts, it's what you think about what you believe – so says the twelfth chapter of Paul's letter to the Romans. Confidence is a mental affirmation of a deep spiritual conviction. It's where our mind says "yes" to our heart.

Deuteronomy 32:30 talks about "one putting a thousand to flight and two putting ten thousand to flight." The first part of that statement affirms that it's amazing what one person can do. You can put a thousand enemies to flight! The second part of the statement is only true when the first is activated. Two "half people" never make a whole. Two inferior, insecure people, working side by side in unity, will not tap the power of synergy or the power of the blessing of God. In fact, things will probably get worse.

The explosive power of unity is not first realised when churches in a city come together – it starts when you come together – mature, complete, lacking nothing (James 1). Unity begins at home, not abroad.

One can put a thousand to flight. There is no better start in life than becoming a "one man band". One man bands have the potential to create interdependent relationships, not co-dependent. Some are joined by bass players. Others aren't.

They don't need to follow convention. They're not desperate for a fuller sound. They love the sound they make.

At every junction in history, God didn't first select a team, a partnership or a choir – He selected an individual. From Abraham to David and from David to Jesus, God chose solitary individuals who found their wholeness in Him and then attracted a team of partners to help them carry the cause.

Your greatest strength is your confidence in the call that was spoken over your life before time began and called you for such a time as this. Song of Songs 4:4 says of the lover, *"Your neck is like the tower of David, built with elegance; on it hang a thousand shields, all of them shields of warriors."* One neck – a thousand shields. Our capacity to carry, conquer, and care for, is much greater than what we think it is. God's intent, through friendly storms, is for us to face our gremlins and overcome our insecurities and inferiorities so that we may become complete individuals who can play brilliant music all on our own.

There are two main kinds of weakness in you. The first kind is "reversible". God replaces our flaws with His strength. His strength rests upon our weaknesses as we cry out to Him. The second kind of weaknesses are "mythical". They don't exist! I'm not weak at the hundred metres sprint – I just don't do it. That's not a weakness, it's a non-strength. Having no "bass player" in a team is not a weakness, it's a non-strength. No teaching gift? That's not a weakness, it's a non-strength. It's time to stop focusing on what you (and your church) can't do and explore the boundaries of what you can do. Think out of the box then get back in the box and explore the outposts of your current strengths. The White Stripes play to their strengths. So much so that you become unaware of their non-strengths. The side effects of having audacious confidence are amazing. I'm not advocating that we completely ignore our non-strengths, but if you spend time strengthening non-strengths, the best that you will ever get is average. On the other hand, if you spend time strengthening your strengths, the best you'll get is genius.

Genius unravelled

No one marries an ugly bride. I've never had a bridegroom turn to me as his bride walks down the aisle and say, "She's a bit ugly, but I'll marry her anyway." Every bride, no matter what shape or size, is beautiful. When the beloved says to his love in Song of Songs 4:1, *"How beautiful you are, my darling! Oh, how beautiful!"* it wasn't a faith statement or a positional statement relating to the cross – it was complete and utter truth – in the eye of the beholder. That's the love language that God's speaking over you right now. That's how God sees you – genius being unravelled from the fishing lines of insecurity and cleansed from the oily waters of sin. There's work to be done, as in marriage, but the bride is beautiful, always and forever. The beloved goes on to describe his bride:

▶ *"Your eyes behind your veil are doves"* (v. 1). Think about it. Your eyes have changed. Once they despised, but now they encourage. Once they glared, but now they forgive. You're beautiful.

▶ *"Your hair is like a flock of goats"* (v. 1). Your strength has returned. You get back up after being knocked down quicker now than you have ever done before. The hair of the Samson church is making a comeback. It didn't go bald, it was only shaved!

▶ *"Your teeth are like a flock of sheep . . . each has its twin"* (v. 2). There's a new cutting edge on your life. You've got zeal on top of wisdom. Perfect balance. Perfect beauty.

▶ *"Your lips are like scarlet ribbon"* (v. 3). The words of your mouth have changed. You're no longer cynical, but expectant.

▶ *"Your temples behind your veil are like the halves of a pomegranate"* (v. 4). Your thoughts are purer and more faithful than they've ever been. You've come a long way. You're awesome!

If we ever want to move into the power of two (putting ten thousand to flight) we need to explore the power of one. Never underestimate the power of one. You are that one – a beautiful bride crafted and changed by God, growing in audacious confidence. Don't stop until you're happy being bass-less. Then add a bass player if necessary.

2. The dream team

If great teamwork holds the key to a great future, how do you go about creating the ideal team? Why is it that the team we have varies greatly from the team we want?!

All of us have made errors in team creation. At times we've panicked in a sincere desire to avoid being seen as a one man band. At other times, our strong desire to see the power of synergy and diversity at work has caused us to unite new-comers to the team far too quickly. All of us want quick growth and at times have cut corners to quickly create a great team, only to regret the decision thereafter. The result is often a divided team of average players instead of a great team of great players.

In church life we have a natural leaning to go for experience over inexperience, old over young, and variety over sameness. But looking at the "Jesus model" of establishing great teams of

great players we see that the first thing our Mentor did was
break all the rules!

Following His remit to choose just twelve team members,
Jesus firstly selected two sets of brothers. In doing so, He used
up four out of twelve precious spaces which could have
included a decent representative from Hebron and a well liked
man from Jerusalem. He also selected four fishermen, ignoring
people from other professions. Is it true that Matthew also
came from the northern part of the country? Did Philip come
from the same town as Peter and Andrew? Can it be right
to show favouritism to Bethsaida? Jesus obviously cut against
the grain of political correctness and rejected the pressure of
representing old and young, black and white, pharmacist and
farmer. Jesus was on course, though, to build the most
important team in history.

In creating a church team we have often veered towards
people with a "deep" understanding of God's word over people
who are shallow, yet incredibly enthusiastic. Is a slightly jaded
ex-Bible college teacher more of an advantage to a team than a
truly excited twenty-year-old? Why do we think that age and
experience is any more helpful to a team than people who are
short in the tooth, got saved three years ago, and never set foot
in any other church?

Many teams are sabotaged by leaders falling for the subtle
demands of the "heavyweights" and the pressure to accommodate all, resulting in a lack of real cohesion, real unity and
real synergy. Theirs is less of a team and more of a collection of
individuals.

The creation of great teams is never instantaneous. I have
outlined four types of team that are all God-ordained, but
not all great. Each has its strengths and each leads to the next
type of team, eventually leading to the possession of a great
team.

(a) Borrowed teams

Often, in coming into a new ministry of opportunities, we are given the team that the previous leader or minister had developed. Sadly the team gradually becomes a dissipating team. The wheels start falling off! The providential purpose of a borrowed team is twofold – firstly it gives the leader a small clearing to plan out what he or she really wants from the new endeavour. It gives a soft start that can help create the superior strategy. Secondly, it gives the leader a chance to have their faith in their God given call a thorough work out. When the team begins to move to other pastures and the leader is left holding the baby, heaven waits to overload the leader with a significant sense of personal destiny. Yes, history has always been changed by individuals first, teams second – individuals who believe that they're born to change their world.

It was Moses who stood in front of the world's greatest leader and said, "Let my people go." It was Gideon who rose from the winepress to raise an army that fought a ludicrous, yet holy, fight. Jonah single-handedly brought revival to Nineveh. And I've made no mention of Martin Luther, Wycliffe and Tyndale. An overriding sense of personal destiny is essential to do outstanding things for God. The team always becomes like its leader. A confident leader, convinced of his call, always creates a confident team convinced of their call. You need a dissipating team!

(b) Scaffold teams

These are the teams you get for quick assembly and a sure start, but don't place too much weight on them. They could be with you for only a limited time.

Scaffold people all look good. All are super enthusiastic and willing to go the extra mile, but there is a mystery that surrounds them. Is their heart as good as their demeanour suggests or is there a major fault line between character and persona?

Often when you first start a new project, you need to take on some people at face value. Their history is erratic, but their desire is positive and you, the leader, have definitely got faith that it's a new day in God. The usual mistake leaders make, though, is to put these "mystery people" into permanent positions that carry some real weight. Scaffold people are just that – scaffold only. Unless you know their heart, you need to use them only for projects that have a start date and a finish date.

Paul told Timothy to entrust what he had to "reliable men" (2 Timothy 2:2) – that always comes down to people with a good track record. In order to juxtapose a "fresh start in faith" with "good track record", it's vital that you only involve these people in short-term projects, not long-term construction. For example, scaffold teams can be assembled for the establishing of a community centre and then dismantled upon completion. Scaffold teams can work the car park rota, but for the next three months only. When true hearts are revealed you can either move them from being "sections of scaffolding" to "stone in the temple", or, if their hearts prove bad, back to the sidelines. Always remember, it is easy to put someone in a position, but really hard to take them out of that position, unless it's pre-arranged through a time limit or tied to a project's completion.

Over half the people who say goodbye to a local church were once totally involved in the life of that church. They often leave because they feel let down by the leadership that promised them "the earth", but failed to deliver when the leadership realised the true state of their heart. The leadership promoted them beyond their heart capacity and allowed them to operate for too long outside of the bounds of their personal relationship with Christ. Often the leader is seduced by their sweet talking words like, "You're the best pastor I've ever had" and, "We just love this church."

Their eventual departure from the local church is often like a coat hook that suddenly shears off from the wall with no prior signs of weakness. It's not a rule (but it's at least 90% true) that when someone repeatedly tells you that they're right behind you, love the vision, think you're the best, can't wait for next Sunday, they're nowhere near ready to be used for the weight bearing construction work of the kingdom. They've just given you the glimpse you needed to see of a heart that's recently questioned you, your vision, the service and all that goes on. Why tell the pastor you're right behind him when it should be obvious?

Scaffold teams are there to give you a good start only. Often, after a good start, a lot of the "to do list" is again placed squarely back in the hands of the leader. Some scaffold will stay on to become significant load bearers while some move on to the next church. Once hearts are revealed, few will remain available to be re-assembled as scaffolding for the next project. The key scripture reference at this time is Philippians 1:6: "God started it, God will complete it!" Good, reliable people are currently being created and called to be a part of the greatest team on earth. That's your team. Believe it! It's a promise that comes by faith!

(c) Foundational teams
Finally – good hearted, proven and happy people! It's what you've been looking for. One heart, one vision, one motive – to do our best for each other and for the King! They love you and want to please Jesus. It's not just functional, it's family. They'll do anything at any time. This is the foundation that God builds His Church on – true servants of the house that have

become true sons of the house. No hirelings here. Sacrifice and surrender are the definitive bedrock.

There is, however, a glitch. It comes to light when you realise that you not only need right character, but also right gifting to get the job done. People may have the passion for the task, but not the best gift. It's disappointing, because this was the team that was to lift the roof off and see thousands added to the church. Frustration leads to friction.

Here's the cruncher – are you more committed to the vision of the house or to the people who are currently in the house? Isn't it the role of a "foundational" team leader not just to attempt to get the job done, but to do a job inside every team member – to find the "divine spark" inside them, disciple them, and then re-position them into places where their real gifting shines. It's going to slow you down, but in the end, for the kingdom as a whole, it will absolutely speed things up.

This is character development time for the leader. Inside all of us is a pragmatist. We just want to see the vision arise, yet God has given us underdeveloped people. Will you love the team as much as you love the vision?

(d) Dream teams

Great teams are not just a God send! Because you've sown into the lives of good-hearted people, God allows you to reap either from your own sowing or from somebody else's sowing. Darlene Zschech once said that the worship team at Hillsong Church in Sydney is selected in the light of how talented each person is. When character is in abundance we can lift our vision off the foundation of the building and onto the construction of the building that uses different materials with different properties for different usages for effective results. Talent and gifting creates the difference between average and brilliant. It's time to believe beyond the foundation of character so that we can add to the strong axe handle a sharp cutting edge.

As Ecclesiastes suggests, when a great team is assembled, less energy is needed by the leader to sustain the team. It's both a happy and a crucial time. If, by the blessing of God, you find you have a great team of great players for the great vision that our great God has given, it must be time to expand your field of dreams. It's time to use up the energy saved by breaking open new territory for the King.

With new territory comes the necessity for new teams. It's here that the cycle begins again. God may give you a borrowed team, then a scaffold team, then a foundational team, then finally a dream team.

3. Mobilising the team

The central aim of every leader isn't just to get vision, but to transfer the vision to the hearts of the people. If the leader's vision becomes every person's vision, the achievement levels will break all records. Vision creation is vital, but vision transfer is essential. Before moving full steam ahead on any programme it's important to spend time and energy imparting vision. Some will never adopt it and in rare occasions, only a few will run with it. For the most part, the majority of the people will be won over and become highly enthusiastic and highly sacrificial members of the greater church team. It will not happen through a single vision Sunday, or by an expensive full colour brochure. It will happen through the creation and mobilisation of four groups of people within your church – vision casters, vision connectors, vision clarifiers and vision carriers.

(a) Vision casters
Casting the vision is the primary call of every leader. It involves

the public proclamation of the next part of the dream and the next stage of the journey for the church and ministry. It's not just a sermon. It's not just a plaque in the entrance foyer. It's laced through every message and every prayer. It's behind every public face and at the heart of ever leader's meeting. Many leaders switch too quickly from getting vision to calling for commitment. By the time the minister announces the vision to the entire church it should already have had time to seep into every person's heart. Press leaks are a vital form of communication that can soften the starkness of the sudden presentation of vision and create a softer landing into people's spirits.

Vision casting is a conscious determination to soak every piece of ground with the declaration of new things to come. In our church we're always casting vision. One day, our assessor for "Investors in People" (a National award for organisational excellence) came to our church building called the Megacentre. He noted that the vision statement wasn't on a plaque or cut into glass in our beautiful foyer. I replied that from the moment he walked in he was met by the vision. It was in the enthusiastic welcome; it was in the colour scheme; it was in the presentation; and it was in the passion expressed in our commitment for Christ. Vision was being carefully cast through everything that could possibly demonstrate it.

(b) Vision connectors

Some people are born to be go-betweens. They're "people" people. We all know them. They're called to take the vision of the principal leader and sell it to the people. They're contagious and energetic. They see every person as a potential carrier and fulfiller of all that the vision contains. They spend their time connecting people with people and people with leaders. They love being the centre of attention and use it to their advantage to personally promote the vision. Despite how well the vision is cast most people don't follow the leader. They follow those who follow the leader. Vision connectors are an essential group of people who both verify the authenticity of the vision and the credibility of the one casting the vision. They seem to turn up in all kinds of places and easily move in and out of a variety of social settings and environments. Smart vision casters always gather vision connectors.

My personality mix is melancholic – choleric. I not only want things done now, but also want things done right. Some of my best team connectors have a sanguine personality type. My preciseness must annoy them and their unstructured-ness sometimes annoys me. I fully realise though that my pragmatic nature, plus their playful nature, creates a great asset in imparting vision to all the people around us.

(c) Vision clarifiers

Casters and connectors all need vision clarifiers. It takes a group of secondary leaders to fully clarify all that the vision entails. They're the people whose gift connects dot to dot. They "flesh it out" and put "meat on the bones". Without the clarifiers, people would be excited, but have no steps to take to see the vision fulfilled.

Clarifiers are strategists. They outline the journey and break it into bite size pieces. For most people, bite size is the right size. They pace the journey without pulling it in a different direction. Clarifiers need to keep perspective and develop their own capacity to see both the macro and the micro at the same time. Without them, much would be lost. My clarifiers tend to be the leaders of management. They lead the teams who look at all the details and potential inner tensions.

Recently, one of my clarifiers said he was torn between the conflict of two budget centres in the life of the church. As he spiralled into the micro, I was able to define the macro and we were together able to define the priorities. His eye for detail was assisted by my eye for perspective. Together, we also make part of a great team.

(d) Vision carriers

Most people in our congregation still have three locks on the front door of their lives. They're in the process of undoing the lock of suspicion, as well as undoing the locks of fear and doubt. Whilst that process is under way, their back door swings open to friends and trusted companions. Vision carriers have the ability to find back doors and be invited in to share friendship and vision. Carriers allow people to window shop their lives and their hearts, allowing people "in" to browse around without necessarily buying what's on offer. They don't sell – they spill. They rub off on people around a relaxed coffee and trade in heavenly commodities. They disarm people. Vision permeates.

Every vision caster and connector needs a band of carriers who will go out amongst the congregation and attract people to the vision. Vision carriers walk completely differently from the way I walk. They tend to mill around while I zoom. Their phlegmatic personality is prone to losing a daily sense of vision and purpose, but is well compensated for by their ability to get into situations that neither cholerics, sanguines, nor melancholics can enter. I live by my diary. They live by a spontaneity which led Jesus to both Zacchaeus and the woman at the well. Together, we make an awesome part of the team.

Vision creation and vision transfer are the essentials of great leadership. Understanding the different functions of vision transfer in your current team can be liberating! Within every good team is a caster, a couple of connectors, at least one clarifier and almost always a few carriers. It's time to fully explore the transfer market!

4. The seven stages of development of team members

New volunteers and staff members that are seconded to be a part of a dynamic and effective team in the life of your church often go through seven stages before the "Team Thing" really clicks and the authority of God clearly emerges. Here's a quick list of the seven stages of team development that they all go through. Allow me to put a humorous slant on it all!

(a) The honeymoon stage
The superhero enters! We've been awaiting this monumental arrival for so long and finally God has supplied. Yippee! Everybody's happy. John Maxwell's books take pride of place on the bookshelf.

(b) The snowed-under stage
The hero has taken on a little more than he can chew. In all of the enthusiasm and testosterone, the pile of work mounts up in his in tray. Snowed under but still smiling!

(c) The crack in the armour stage
Nobody's perfect! What did you expect – a real superhero? The cracks start showing as he starts to operate outside of his capacity and gifting. Stiff upper lip ensues. Slight distancing emerges as you take a reality check on Mr Invincible.

(d) The martyr stage
"It's unfair!" ... "Nobody cares" ... "I'm doing all the work around here!" ... "I was promised support" ... "I don't think I like him." All images and impressions are well and truly shattered. A love-hate relationship develops. A ratty attitude is evident. Loss of motivation, joy and energy are all apparent.

(e) The personal crisis stage

Mr "Nine spiritual gifts wrapped up into one exciting package" has a crisis of calling, confidence, attitude and faith. He finally cracks. Emotions fly high, sparks rise and a cry to heaven results. A sense of call is reaffirmed and the peace of God transcends. A sense of love, acceptance and forgiveness wraps itself around the non-productive, exhausted team member.

(f) The redefinement stage

A heart to heart creates a relationship deeper than ever before. They saw how you never rejected them, even when productivity was jeopardized by wrong attitude. A reduction of workload follows as the portfolio is reduced to areas of the team member's strength.

(g) The high productivity stage

Talent, anointing, unity and right-heartedness all begin to flow to produce a team member who is now brimming with high efficiency, high authority and high fulfilment.

Teamwork is brilliant when the team works for the common good of the fulfilment of the vision. It's important not to rush into the power of team, but to allow the team to grow and develop in an organic and natural way. As hearts are knit through being "on the same page", and as gifts begin to make room and space for themselves, the amazing power of team dynamics begins to rise up, resulting in great conquests and achievements.

Understanding leadership, management and grass roots ministry

In many churches, people who succeed at grass roots ministry find that their success takes them on to the leadership team of the church. They then find themselves moving from competency to incompetency because they are now way out of their depth. Everyone struggles and bad times loom. In a lot of churches, people involved in management love to dabble in leadership, without realising that they've crossed the line from being the facilitators of vision to being the creators of it. Too many cooks really do spoil the broth. Many senior leaders spend so much of their time on their favourite grass roots ministry, or the squeaky wheel, or on management issues, that the gift of leadership lies either neglected or invaded by people who should have nothing to do with it. The result is that churches lack the wisdom, insight and skills needed to mobilise the army into their own giftings and purposes. The "do it all" pastor often misses the mark by a mile.

A great church is one where *leadership*, *management* and *ministry* are each clearly defined and each fully mobilised. Most people in core leadership operate in all three areas but, without clear definition and knowledge, they can easily ignore their primary gift of leadership. Busyness looks great, but can keep churches very small indeed. It's the squeaky wheel that gets most of the attention in many churches and many leaders are seduced into spending all of their time on the shop floor. They then begin to neglect the ministry of oversight and, in so doing, fail to properly manage the details of all that has been initiated. Projects designed to produce great momentum are neglected for the cries of those who need caring for. The root causes of dissatisfaction, disassociation and dissention are never really solved because leadership is never properly developed.

I am continuing to learn that time to hone the craft of leadership is essential to my church's success. Life in our church has a maddening pace and a diversity of operation that can be daunting. Just a few years ago my office was in the middle of all this activity. We run an indoor play centre six days a week, a conference and concert venue, a full-time Bible training school that has now become the Audacious Academy, and community programmes, as well as all of the other activities that make up church life. My eye for detail regularly drove me crazy as I got involved in every nook and cranny of the organisation.

The paradigm change came initially through employing a faithful church member as our Operations Manager. No longer was there a direct link between myself and all of the daily management duties. I moved my office to my house. I can still be obsessively detailed and occasionally let rip – firstly to keep everyone on their toes with regards to our visionary quest for quality in all we do, and secondly because I am yet to totally master my obsessiveness (maybe that should come first!). The advantage, though, is that it has given me more time with God, more time looking for wisdom, more authority from God and more strategic involvement in the deepening and refining of our great vision for our future.

The New Testament reveals this demarcation between church leadership and church management by the setting aside of a management team in Acts chapter 6. Seven men released the Apostles to more prayer, more preaching, and a quicker establishment of the "Apostles doctrine". In Ephesians chapter 4 we see a demarcation between "Ascension" gift ministry and those who do "the work of the ministry". Without the "gift" ministry which involves character development, spiritual direction and impartation, grass roots ministry is always thwarted and never fully prepared for the outworking of the ministry. Here are some defining characteristics of leadership, management and ministry:

▶ **Leadership** looks upon the whole church (or department) it oversees. It looks towards the future. It charts the course and motivates, equips and strategizes so others can follow. If leadership is the rudder, then management is the engine.

▶ *Management* enables and orchestrates. It takes the plans to fill in the details. It looks inward while leadership looks outward. It helps put the right people in the right places. It troubleshoots and finds practical solutions to release leaders and grass roots ministries. It joins the dots together to make a glorious picture. It organises systems and teams and sets goals in the realm of probability (all that lies between what is and what could be).

▶ *Ministry* causes God's Spirit to lift up the afflicted, save the sinner, and bring release to the captives. When leadership and management abound, grass roots ministry goes ballistic. It's specific and sharp. It's empowered and resilient.

Try not to sweep the floors (and clean the loos!)

Most ministers don't fully believe that their leadership is a serving role. They serve the flock as overseers. They were actually called against their will by the overriding will of God to a position of responsibility that, in essence, is pure servanthood. Many leaders don't see that and spend their time proving their servanthood to the congregation by cleaning floors and loos and setting out seats. In so doing they can actually work against the heart of servanthood by not releasing those who are called to cleaning. There is no difference between cleaning and preaching – both are a form of serving. When that fact is settled the church will come alive. Setting an example is important, but ignoring your service in "leadership" is suicide. In all the confusion we've invented the term "servant leader". It's like calling someone a "rowing oarsman" or a "front of plane pilot". Humility is a heart issue, not a job profile. As each part of the body serves with their God-given gifts in their particular calling, success will be imminent.

If ministers could see this they would stop feeling so guilty for not serving more and stop trying to do the stuff everybody else is meant to do. Jesus certainly went about doing good and healing the oppressed. His primary role, though, was to "strengthen the strong" so that they would eventually "strengthen the weak". His primary investment was in His core twelve. Many local churches and many denominations ignore the strong and go straight for the weak. If you meet every need you'll eventually burn out! Jesus wisely said, "The poor you'll always have." If you put demand above strategy you'll end up out of control, yet being in control is one of the freedoms that Christ won for us on the cross. It's the ability not to be pulled aside by fear, guilt and denial, but to strategically build upon God-given principles.

The best way to go about this change of priorities, as well as the way you spend your time, is to firstly fill your diary with the stuff of discipleship. Secondly, you need to put in other God-directed opportunities, and thirdly, you need to leave some space for everything else. The "important, but not urgent" then takes pole position over the "urgent, but not important".

It's time to put the Leadership Pyramid the right way up, with leadership on top, management in the middle, and grass roots ministry on the bottom. In turning it upside down we can lessen the idea that oversight comes from above, not below. It's a biblical paradigm. Because servanthood exists equally in each person, you cannot use a triangular pyramid (upside down or side on) to represent it.

Let the leaders lead, the managers manage, and the people minister. If you're involved in all three then acknowledge what you're doing and why you're doing it so that the real needs of the church are never neglected. It's time to get the big things right and take our place in providing vision, resource, motivation and wisdom for all who are placed under our care.

Essential leadership kit
(to create great partnership for the journey)

- Partnership begins with you. The more complete you become, the more powerful your team will become. Never underestimate the power of one.
- Your current team may be a foundational team, not a dream team. Make sure you know who you've got so you can tailor your leadership accordingly.
- Vision isn't just thought, it's caught. Get the vision out through casting, connecting, clarifying and carrying it right to the edge of church life.
- Remember great teams and great team members aren't developed overnight!

The Diary Archives

1st May 1999
I've had a revelation about God's affection and love for me that has been awesome. I'm really beginning to understand God's heart for me to succeed and His heart to rid me of sinful habits. I'm starting to understand God's immense affection towards me and His incredible delight over those who choose to follow Him. I don't want this revelation ever to depart! It really enables me to love myself so much more and to love others a lot more as well.

Looking back, it seems that we spent a lot of our time from halfway through 1996 to halfway through 1998 training and consolidating all the new, upcoming leadership of our church. Many are a lot younger than those who left in our season of crisis. Halfway through last year we planted our new leadership into the new fields of ministry. So many are just starting to see buds of life. I feel so happy leading such a talented and gifted team of leaders. Behind each leader are some fantastically dedicated teams. These are good days in the life of the church. The church is growing slowly, but surely, and I'm continuing to grow in depth and anointing.

I was amazed at my renewed heart for this city. I was reading this morning Zechariah's prophecies about the renewal of Jerusalem – kids playing freely on the streets, the over seventies all revelling in new found safety . . . I realised afresh God's plans for this great city – to release freedom, life and safety and to bring prosperity both to the soul and to the streets. I feel a new authority upon me to speak into the life of leaders in the city and the nation. I'm staggered as I have always seen myself as a second in charge when it comes to anything wider than our local church.

We recently had a financial report completed by Anne, my financial assistant. For the first time, I think, in the history of the church, we hit our monthly target without any exceptional offerings. Miracles do happen! In fact, with the inclusion of some extra funding we have received, we have potentially paid off every bill that is owed (outside our mortgage and the personal loan that someone has graciously lent us). I'm astonished! Especially since it's come to pass at the beginning of the new year, which is usually a time of tightening the belt after the Christmas season. We have a huge budget and have always stretched ourselves beyond our ability. It has caused many stresses and strains and this all comes as a welcome break. I am now really challenged to put the wages up for the staff and raise the bar on our budget forecast! We need to bless our core workers more. Everyone has sacrificed *so* much.

I've been keeping this journal of "The Sheffield Revival" for just over a year now. We still haven't seen the "Revival" yet, but it's in our hearts and it's in our speech. We're not over desperate for it, knowing that great oaks start with small acorns.

We have made a commitment to walk by faith and at the weakest times we've declared our strengths. I remember on the fourth Sunday at the start of the church, with only about twelve people present, declaring "Hope" (our church was originally called "The Hope of Sheffield") to be an "Antioch church" influencing nations. We'll continue to do it. I'm dedicated to declaration. So much foundation is in place; so many leaders are in their right position. Zechariah says that God rejoices to see the "plumb-line in the hands of Zerubbabel" – in other words, the right leadership in place at the right time. I declared yesterday to the congregation that you won't find "the Hope" at the Megacentre in ten years time! You'll find a community centre and the church in the community, but our Sunday meetings will be too big to fit our new downstairs auditorium. I think they're getting used to big talking! I refuse to be tempered by past or current failures to come up with high results. Goals are important, but I know that our future lies in the spirit of faith rather than the attainment of current goals. We're still believing for great breakthrough, but we can smell the fresh breeze that hopefully will lead to a cyclone of God's power and purposes.

9th May 1999

I'm in the middle of a nine day fast. God has really spoken to me regarding the sense that I'm moving into a new season with Him. I've just had around three months of incredible intimacy and coming to tears almost every time I spend time with Him. One of the city ministers said that I need to "pioneer a course to a new watering hole", which got me thinking that maybe my current season of revelation was coming to an end. I read the story of Jesus on the Mount of Transfiguration. It said that when they came to the bottom of the mountain there was a large crowd waiting for them.

God spoke to me and said that you can't continually live on the mountain top. There's a crowd waiting to be ministered to and a generation ready to be reached. It gave me impetus to start to fast again and seek a greater anointing to impact the harvest. His purpose for me now is to minister horizontally after a great season of being ministered to vertically! I cried the other night when I felt His presence was not the same as it had been so strongly for months. I didn't want it to go and felt really upset. Just to know His immediate affection and concern for a long period was a real taste of heaven. It's as if God has purposefully pushed me back out into the harvest field. There's a call to take up God's authority in prayer and rise up and possess the land. Why can't God bring revival to Sheffield?

God is beginning to speak to me about my leadership style. I have a hand in everything and need to learn to do things through my leaders and not go behind them. Secondly, I need to keep things vision based and not job based. I see the ideal and probably put too much emphasis upon my ideas and my standards of excellence. I need to give time to letting the garden grow and not check out the roots so often. I've been in town today and picked up some picture frames to give as presents for people at church. I then felt to put them down. This was a job for delegation. Father, help me also to be good at delegating!

16th May 1999

After tucking myself away for the past three years, Mal Fletcher of "Next Wave International" prophesied a re-expansion of myself into the heart of mission. He said that it was a key to my church's strength and future and he's invited me to a leadership summit in Oslo, Norway. Someone prophesied that as I gave out from the church, God would give back to it.

There's a new confidence and a new level of anointing on me as I've been ministering out from our church. I used to hate preaching in other places. I seem now to have a mandate to lift people's hope and expectancy to new levels and I have a number of messages that help do that. I have enjoyed ministry lately!

On a really personal note, I have found myself wrestling with temptations, especially with lust of the eyes. It's a growing concern. I have prayed about it and that same person who prophesied over me regarding God blessing our church as I ministered out, also warned me not to do anything that dissolves or removes the anointing of God's Spirit. They then looked me in the eyes and said, "Do you know what I mean?" Amazing! It's broken the back of my problem. In fact, I feel clean, free and fearful of God. Anything that may feed the flesh I'm running from. It's as if a stronghold has been broken. I know that God has rescued me from a slippery path leading to destruction. I thank my Lord so much for His commitment and care towards my life. I can really understand how people (and ministers) fall into immorality – even those with good marriages. I can now really understand what a dirty and dark world people live in who are trapped by the devil's temptations. I want to run from the plains of compromise. I want to be holy for all my living years. God, help it be so.

Reinhard Bonnke Has No Higher Calling Than You

The Confusion of Calling

Far more people start races than finish them! I can recall my Bible college class and recount many people who failed to keep going on the journey of faith. They may have been exhausted, discouraged, or simply looking for God to do more than He was doing. It seems that the difference between those who succeeded and those who stopped didn't lie in their difficulties, but in their dispositions. Those who succeeded didn't have more than those who failed – they simply did more with the little they had.

All of my Christian life I held a notion that the Body of Christ was made up of loads of "one talent" people, some "two talent" people, and a few "five talent" people. Not much was really expected from the single talented ones, but from the five talented ones (like me), much was expected. It was a hard call, but heck, someone had to do it!

From a quick read of Matthew 25 it would appear that my thinking was spot on – five talents were given to one person, two to another, and one to the guy who was just exercising a bit of faithfulness with one measly measure. From a more careful read of Matthew 25 it would appear that after a distinct period of time, the 5, 2 and 1 talents become 10, 4 and 1, and then they become 11, 4 and 0 talents. The five talent man had become the eleven talent man while the one talent man was left with nothing.

In this chapter we're going to look at the truth that it's not what you've got that counts in leadership – it's what you do with what you've got, and how being exhausted can actually be a good thing!

Increasing your "talent capacity"

I had equated the handing out of talents (resources) intrinsically with the callings of God: for example, Jack Hayford has to be a five talenter, while some of those who work in his church office are probably just one talenters. Upon a serious look at Matthew 25, it became evident that God matched resources less to calling than to ability. In other words, God gives according to our ability to handle what He gives us (Matthew 25:15). If our ability to handle what God gives us is small, then He will match that with some small degree of resource. He won't continue to pour into a full vessel no matter what size it is. The volume and strength of the vessel determines its ability, and its ability determines what it receives, whether it be 5, 2 or 1 talent.

For years I believed that the "higher" the calling, the greater the number of "talents" given to match it. I believed it until I asked myself the question, "Does Jack need more faith or less faith than Lucy to run his influential international ministry?" After all, Lucy's primary responsibility is attached to the photocopier – day in, day out, week in, week out. The correct answer to this question is neither more nor less. Jack and Lucy are both called to walk by faith – end of story. Does Jack need strength? Surely it takes more strength at times to follow the leader than to be the leader (so my wife says). But then, surely

God has given much more to Jack. But if you saw how broken Lucy was just before she got saved then God's definitely given more to Lucy. Or has He?

The real answer to the differences in the "measures" God gives isn't found in calling. It's found in capacity. God is a God of the "increasing measure" (2 Peter 1). If our capacity increases then our ability to receive increases. If we use what God gives us well, then we'll be given more. If we don't, God will cut down the supply. Usage increases capacity, increasing both talents given and talents created. Our current ability, therefore, is defined by our stewardship of our previously gained God-given resources. Our future ability is defined by our current stewardship with today's God-given resources. If we're diligent and faithful to what God has given us today, we will move up from two talents to four to eight to sixteen etc. – an exponentially increasing amount, possibly in this life, definitely in the next. There is only one limit to what God can do – the limitation of our capacity. This is all great news.

When people look at me from the pews they think that my excelling is all a part of my call. They think, "Well, that's what leaders do!" They think that high activity, high energy, high finances, high spirits and high passion are all a part of the high call. Not true. It's not a part of the call, it's a part of the capacity. And so it is with every person. All of us start with a low number, usually one. What we do with "one" determines our two, five, ten, twenty etc. Every calling needs increasing amounts of distinct resourcing from heaven. Every calling needs to be equally reliant upon the treasury of heaven and equally diligent with heaven's current down-payments.

Don't mistake this as arrogance. I believe that I'm not only currently living my life – I'm also living a number of other people's lives as well. In Jesus' parable, the talent was taken from the man who had just one and placed in the hands of the man who now had ten: *"For everyone who has will be given more"* (Matthew 25:29). Who was it that failed to rise up in their God-given call by failing to be faithful and zealous with all that God had given them? Who was it that downsized their one talent as they gazed in envy at those who had five? Who was it who hid behind a myriad of excuses and buried their talent, only to be retrieved by the Giver and reinvested in me? What parts of my life are the re-birthing of gifts that lay dormant and unexercised in the lives of others? Who knows? (Only God!) The reason I'm making this point is simply to heat the air with sobriety and cause a new wind of accountability to blow – accountability to God for what He's currently invested in and banking on in our personal and church lives.

In view of all of this, a corporate truth emerges. Our churches may not actually be limited by the number of talented people around, or by the number of people who really know the word of God! They may not be limited by a so-called "closed heaven" or a lack of prayer. They are limited by their true size – the size of their capacity. An open heaven may prove largely wasted when the vessel is tiny and the aperture small.

Our church's capacity is determined by our church's use of the resources currently available from heaven. If that is the bottom line then it's time to stop waiting for a crop of highly talented and highly spiritual individuals to suddenly drop in to populate our churches. As "everyone who has" is diligent with what they possess, they "will be given more" and focusing upon the exercising of talents, gifts and resources should open the door to an increase from heaven for the current participants. It should also open the door to the future inclusion of people who are what your church really needs. God will give more to the church that uses more of what it already has. Excellence is not about getting the best – it's about being the best. Why? Because it leads to the "increasing measure" that is currently being held in the heavenly storeroom for you.

In looking at the seven possible downfalls of the one talent man who lost everything we can ascertain seven ways to increase our share of heaven's resources to become even more effective for our King and country.

1. Never despise the day of small beginnings

Never "downsize" your one talent by comparing it to five talents. Everyone begins with one. Who knows what may become of us if we're faithful in little.

2. Never confuse calling for capacity

Everyone needs to exhume treasure from heaven. Everyone needs an equally abundant slice of heaven to live up to being more than conquerors. If you're travelling the Amazon for lost tribes, you need faith. If you're travelling across town to "Little Tykes" nursery, you also need faith. The Bible says, "The just (that's everyone) shall live by faith"!

3. Never think that God has favourites

There's no favouritism either in this parable or in that of the minas (Luke 19:12–27). Each person was given an identical amount. It's not what you get that counts, it's what you do with what you get that determines your success.

4. Never work off reputation, work off revelation

Our one talent man hid it in the ground. If his master had a reputation for being "tight" it certainly wasn't evident in this parable. Enthusiasm and zeal are the bi-product of an ever widening revelation of the nature of God. They that "know their God shall do mighty exploits" (see Daniel 11:32).

5. Never take a vision and give back a job

The vision was one of investment and growth. The final encounter was the return of a bag full of coins. Make sure that you hand out vision, stir up vision, and talk up vision. Never let a vision become a job.

6. Never allow laziness to clothe itself

Our one talent man was lazy. Lazy people love the chase, but haven't the inclination to roast the game they catch (it's somewhere in Proverbs, but I can't be bothered to find it). These people are at the start, but never at the finish. It's a capacity killer! It's time to expose it and accept nothing less than maximum effort.

7. Never accept less than "Well done, good and faithful servant."

- *Well* = excellence by choice. I will do the best I can with faith.
- *Done* = I will do whatever it takes.
- *Good* = humility before honour. I will keep my attitude right.
- *Faithful* = enduring in faith.
- *Servant* = called to serve. I will serve and refresh others.

It's not according to favouritism and it's not according to calling. It's according to our capacity for increased capacity. Let's make that a driving ambition. Use what you have in your hand today and God will give you more. That's for sure.

Exhausted? That's good!

Some time ago I put out a fatwa amongst my staff and core team: From now on when asked, "How are you?" we're not going to say, "I'm so tired!" It became like a broken record down what were supposed to be the corridors of power! If God's going to increase our capacity, He must firstly bring us to a place of exhaustion. It's a prerequisite for the expansion of our capacity in God. "Exhaustion" seems like a bad word in Christian circles.

Exhaustion has appeared on the stage of ministry as an unwelcome intruder. To be worn out, whacked out, worked up, and wrung out, seems to be bad news. But is it? A lot of leaders complain all the time that they're tired and weary, but is that one of the conditions that accompanies a life that's out of sync with the will of God, or is it one of the conditions that accompany a life that's completely in sync with scaling the heights of destiny and shaping our world?

In the book of Ruth, Naomi declares, *"I went away full, but the LORD has brought me back empty"* (Ruth 1:21). Was it such a bad thing? In 2 Timothy, Paul declares, *"For I am already being poured out like a drink offering . . . "* (2 Timothy 4:6). Was that a recipe for a nervous breakdown? Being emptied, spent, done in, and fed up are, in fact, all excellent places to be. For precisely the following Top 10 reasons!

1. You've got to be empty to be filled

Simply put, you've got to use all you have before God will give you more. We want to hang on to a little bit of yesterday's manna because we don't believe in a brand new day's provision. Blessed are the "poor in spirit", the bereft and the exhausted! Because the last of what we have is as important as the first of what we have (it's harder to give away your last fruit pastel than your first two!). It's the very last morsel of our energy that needs to remain dedicated to the pursuit of God. Often people encourage us to hold on to three free nights a week and make them ours. Or, if they see us with bags under our eyes, to have a holiday. Our culture is a culture of rewarding ourselves! If you dare to spend yourself on behalf of the needy (and replace

complaining with complete faith in God's provision), watch out!
Your light's about to explode as God fills you with light and
glory for all to see (Isaiah 58:10).

2. It's our utmost for His highest

Don't ever die with potential still in your heart. It's fine to say
to a thirty-year-old, "You've got potential," but it seems odd to
say it to a fifty-five-year-old. Why? Because the older we get, the
faster we run, holding nothing back for a rainy day, believing
that all we have and own has been lent to us by our Lord. The
first of all we have is both the first and the last.

3. The end of the natural is the beginning of the supernatural

Job 42:10 says, *"After Job had prayed for his friends, the LORD made
him prosperous again . . . "* After the smallest of all his concerns
had been exhausted, the Lord turned the page. The King James
Version states it even more dramatically: *"The LORD turned the
captivity of Job, when he prayed for his friends."* When the last of
the bread was broken, the miracle started to flow – 5,000 in one
encounter.

4. Prove your faith is alive

Faith without works is still dead – as much today as it ever was.
Buoyancy is the evidence of great faith. A hive of activity should
be the description of every local church. If you believe it, you'll act
upon it. Action means high energy, and that means exhaustion –
ready to be filled again and again with the energy of heaven.

5. Demonstrate your devotion

Ask any team member of any entrepreneurial company that has
a desire for world dominion and they'll tell you they're always
tired! That's life for motivated people: tired, but loving every

minute of it. Christians that are too light-footed may be a little divorced from full devotion. To be whacked out in your love for Christ and people demonstrates the magnitude of the greatest cause on earth.

6. You're on the brink of a miracle

"Weeping may remain for a night ... but rejoicing comes in the morning" (Psalm 30:5). When the brook runs dry there's a miracle with the woman at Zarephath waiting. Your faith is the key to your future. Faith always bleeds hope and expectation when cut with the knife of crisis. Right now you may need two weeks alone in the Bahamas, but having your spirit replenished is of even greater value – and it's coming. Stressed? Let Jesus take the load and keep it. "My expectation is in Him!"

7. God exalts the humble

To be full of oneself is to live a life of crime. To be emptied through a life of "grime" by lifting up the lowly is a life that's loved by heaven. Self-protection, self-confidence, self-esteem, self-worth, self-consciousness and rewarding oneself are all full of self. Teach your people to cross the line to complete dependency upon God. Influence and authority awaits!

8. Exhausted people have the best holidays

Work hard, play hard! The bane of the lazy is to not unwind because they haven't been wound. To have the best holiday you need to go into it having given your all to the world around you. Too many ministers live a life of leisure!

9. The Church grows because of you

Ephesians 4:16 states *"... as each part does its work ... "* Work implies a depletion of energy resources. The promise is that the body "grows and builds itself up" as a result of hard work. Jesus asks us to pray for "labourers" for the harvest field. That implies work – the hard work of "compelling" them to come to Jesus. What a result! Exhausted? That's good!

10. Great is your reward in heaven

"I have fought the good fight, I have finished the race, I have kept the faith. Now there is in store for me a crown of righteousness..." (2 Timothy 4:7–8). Although that is the greatest of our rewards, it's not the end of them. Stop siding with the unadventurous people who have allowed their Christianity to simmer and smoulder. Stir up the energies of the Spirit, step out into the unexplored, and cast your eyes towards eternity. Great shall your reward be.

The greater your capacity the more God can give to you and flow through you. Psalm 16:6 says, *"The boundary lines have fallen for me in pleasant places."* God doesn't want the boundaries of our lives to fall in the gullies of exhaustion or the cliffs of incompetence. He wants to take you far beyond today's capacity into a place only limited by His will and destiny. Pleasant places! As we break through onto higher ground, so shall every person that we lead.

Essential leadership kit
(to create stamina for the journey)

- Life isn't about what you've been given. It's about what you do with what you've been given.
- God gives more vision to people currently exercising vision – you could fulfil more than just your destiny in your lifetime!
- If you're tired – do it tired. Exhaustion can take you over the line from self-reliance to the magnificence of God-reliance, where real faith is both released and activated.

The Diary Archives

14th January, 2000

It's the 21st Century. I'm sitting in the Novotel Hotel preparing my message for Sunday. It takes me so long to get inspired. I go through so much agony in preaching. I'm called to preach, but it's not something that comes easily. I find it so hard to churn out messages (like some do) and really admire those who can just get up and talk so easily and freely. For me, sermon preparation is like pulling teeth!

The wave that we recently saw in church growth has now retracted again. I really dislike waves. Nevertheless, I have a renewed fire and passion to kick the year into touch with some fervent prayer and some regular fasting. As soon as the New Year turned, I felt a renewed determination to pray and to go public in declaring God's promise all over again to the congregation. I want to see many more people come in than go out; I want to see devotion and dedication like never before. I'm declaring, "This is my year." I'm back into battle after having such a massive revelation in 1998 of God's favour and calling towards my life.

Because of the turbulent nature of the demands on our resources, we still have been unable to adequately set up a full budget forecast for all of our operations. We spend all we get and, as we are so far out of our depth, a complete budget would be purely academic. We can't continue like this. Our underlying financial situation is constantly in the red (yet, we have never gone under). We are being sustained by God, but it's more wilderness living than Canaan living. Despite all of this, and in response to all of this, my assistants and the financial panel have decided to massively increase my wages in line with a prophetic word from a minister based in America. He told Dave and Glyn that the church must honour its leadership in the same way as the Ten Commandments instruct us to honour our mother and father. He inferred that the church will always be in lack unless this tangible honour is put in place. If the church honours leadership, God will honour and bless the church.

It's been a gutsy step and the strain has increased more now that the decision has been made. We are however, believing our Lord and see it as a key to the blessing of God. Our faith has also increased. We've had two visits from Sheffield City Council in the last week – one reviewing their partnership in the creation of a "Mega Gym" and the other to lease floor space. It's slightly strange how, in the midst of our great daily needs, we have two incredible possibilities concerning our long-term needs. The leasing has the potential to stabilise the whole centre and put us in a position to borrow finance to complete our 700-seater auditorium.

In three weeks we're aiming to raise £250,000 from our congregation. It's called our "Full House" offering for our new auditorium. I really hope it succeeds. We don't need a miracle offering as much as a heart miracle as people get hold of the vision and put their whole weight behind it. We're looking for alabaster jar type giving! I've told the church not to pray too much about what to give! The woman with the alabaster jar wasn't necessarily prompted by the Holy Spirit, but prompted by an incredible appreciation and devotion to God. She gave out of being "truly, madly and deeply" in love with Jesus. In asking God how much to give to Him we run the risk of taking the spirit of love out of our expression of love towards Him. I believe in listening to the Holy Spirit, but often He's there to tell us when to stop, rather than when to start! I want people to go beyond the bottom line as well as beyond the normal "business" agreement with God of giving in order to get. This is to be all about love.

The amazing thing that I've learnt about an alabaster jar is that you can't unscrew the lid – it can only be smashed off. You can't give in half measure! Already, I've heard of a car being sold and a wedding being downsized to offer the Lord the financial savings. We're really trusting in the Lord. There seems to be a lot going on in the Spirit realm, rippling into relationships and the general atmosphere. I believe that the offerings being made will guarantee us awesome victories.

Today's update:
The "Mega Gym" never got off the ground. We needed the same space for our youth and children's work and the Council were endlessly delayed by too many focus groups.

3rd March, 2000
We had our "Full House" offering (to be redeemed in the next three months) and it totalled £140,000. We were a little taken back – we expected more. I've had to realise that, over the past few years, the people have given, above normal offerings (and including this offering), up to £300,000 towards the work.

Our offering was all about what we could do for God. We're now in the territory of seeing what God can do for us. We have enough to get started, but not enough to finish. We've seen the architect and we've got the ball rolling. We need to receive £80,000 of the "Full House" offering in the next seven weeks to get the place ready in time for Alive 2000 Conference in October. Help Lord! Then we need another £250,000 to internally equip the place. It's incredible that we've got the possibility of Adrian Plass coming in November and have even been asked to hire the auditorium for a week in November by Soul Survivor. The pressure's on! I feel nervous! I feel that our name is at stake as we've publicly stated our intentions that all will be completed in time. I can think of a few alternative plans, but I've refused to talk about them or entertain them. I'm applying faith principles and trusting in the Lord. I know that today I'm a day closer to a miracle! The word of God is full of them – outstanding breakthroughs of God when the people had done all they could.

There's a good feel at church at the moment. I feel like we're on the start of a growth curve. It's only a feeling, but I think that it's a "God feeling". We've had some excellent meetings. There's good momentum. Youth are getting saved and we're moving towards our goal of "2148" – sharing something of the gospel to 2 people each week, inviting 1 person to a church event each month, seeing 4 decisions in our main meeting each week, and baptising 8 people each month. It's a huge goal, but we're aiming high.

Jenny put on an excellent national women's event this week. She began these events with fifty ladies a couple of years ago and last year it jumped to eighty ladies attending. This week she had one hundred and sixty ladies in attendance with a lot of leaders among them. It's a move of God in our midst. It's exciting. Jen still has problems with her eating. She finds that red meat and anything spicy causes her stomach to bloat, resulting in great pain. It's been happening for the past year. She sometimes wakes up at two or three in the morning with stomach pain that almost causes her to pass out.

I've found that reading the Bible at McDonalds really works for me. Even with the radio on, I find that I can still focus on the word! I work well with "consistent" distraction rather than "inconsistent" distraction! Since last August I've come to McDonalds almost every day after a morning run. I then go for a prayer walk to walk off the McMuffin! It's a great routine – I really enjoy it and find that it really releases me.

I'm at McDonald's right now being reminded that I'm writing the diary of the Sheffield Revival – something that is as unknown as rain was to Noah. I've only told Jenny about this diary. That's why I'm alive – for revival. That's why I'm here. I've not got to forget the big picture – it's about the gospel impacting lives and impacting a nation.

I turned forty a few weeks ago. It's old! No one who's older believes that, but everyone younger does! I've got to realise that it really is quite old, so I don't subconsciously create an "ageing congregation". Many forget to raise up the next generation because they still think they're young. My mother is now in her seventies. My wife says that it's not old! My mum says it's not old! It's all relative.

With Dave and Anne becoming part-time missionaries, I'm now looking for a pastor to run our pastoral care. I think I've had a paradigm shift from the necessity to have an older person. When I was eighteen, twenty-six was old! I'm open to raising up the next generation in a big way. I also know that what they may lack in experience, we'll gain in teachability and examplehood!

CHAPTER 5

Bring Back Personality Driven Churches

The Confusion of Charisma

There is a divine spark inside each of us! Don't quote me on this – it's a quote from *Bruce Almighty*. Bruce had spent a frustrating percentage of his life trying to be what he wasn't. Bruce (played by Jim Carey) was the "light entertainment" correspondent of the nightly newscast, yet in his insecurity, he wanted to be seen in a more serious light.

His quest for the prestigious position of anchorman led to horrible consequences for the entire world! God (played by Morgan Freeman) had a heart to heart with Bruce and revealed to him that deep within him lay a divine spark. Bruce's God-given spark was bringing laughter and happiness to the world. He "saw the light" and set about finding and becoming himself – content, funny and furious!

In this chapter, we'll be looking at how to release the incredible power of originality that's locked up within you and in the church; how to not take yourself so seriously; and how heaven is not as serious as you think!

The power of originality

If Abba reunited they'd make megabucks, yet "Bjorn Again", the Australian Abba tribute band who sing better, play better, and look younger, only make thousands. Why is that? It's the power of originality.

It's the same for you and your church. Why would the devil spend time undermining your incredible God-given gift of personality? Why do we admonish a "cell driven" church, a "purpose driven" church, a "passion driven" church, yet vilify a "personality driven" church? Why is a church allowed to be led by strong leadership, but not strong charisma? Who made charisma so superficial and so "American"? Is there a power at work to weaken the power that's generated where originality abounds? (Cue the *Jaws* theme tune now!)

The funny thing about leaders and ministers is that they often change personalities upon entering the pulpit. It's a unique morphing that I've been guilty of many times over. The result is a pale imitation of someone else's divine spark.

So much of our life owes its power to the power of originality. Take faith for example. Faith comes by an original word from God. You can't just repeat a verse from the Bible and then try to believe it. Either you believe it or you don't. You can't fake it. When God speaks, faith is ignited. It's not borrowed faith, nor humanly generated. It doesn't come through the laying on of hands. It comes via the power of ignited originality.

The gifts of the Spirit also operate on the strength of originality. They express themselves with unique words for a unique season and plan. And they do it through personality.

It's also a funny thing to see what happens when many people prophesy. Their voice changes, their manner changes, and for whatever intents and purposes, they become a "different" person. Who devalued and disfigured the vessel through which the gifts would operate?

The power of originality can be best expressed by the releasing of four types of "power" from within you.

1. The power of the real you

Inside each of us is a unique gift – it's the way we're wired. Each of us has individual wiring that leads to different types of expression. It's true that sin has distorted parts of the real us, but it's also important never to throw the baby out with the bathwater.

As a child I spent many long hours trying to win national competitions in science, Lego building and writing. Time and time again I would spend a great deal of effort trying to be the first caller through to Melbourne's premier radio station. I often won competitions because I had pre-dialled every number bar the last. As a teenager I spent many long hours inventing ways to break into concerts and socials. Three times I gained entry to see Elton John – each time ticket-less! Now, everything I've just mentioned deals with a particular gift I have (some of you would find that hard to believe!) The problem was not the gift. It was the application of the gift. Although, when it came to breaking into concerts, it was used inappropriately, it was an awesome entrepreneurial gift at work.

When I got saved I adopted a more conservative approach to life – contrary to who I was. I ran from the past with disdain, not just for what I used to do, but for who I used to be. In my desire for holiness I not only abandoned the bathwater, but the baby as well. I became "beige". And that's where the story begins and ends. Churches without colour, charisma, curiosity, and creativity, are squeezed into the mould of religious conservatism or wholesale impersonation (when I get older I'll get an opinion!).

2. The power of charisma

Train spotting is a quirky British pastime. Wrapped up in their anoraks wearing coke bottle glasses, we can't think of anyone or anything more "boring!" Sure, a TV show about trains may not be prime time, but a programme about train spotters could very well be prime time. Why? Because train spotters have **charisma**! There is a unique energy that drives them to spend hours watching out for trains. That energy is the power of originality at work through the letting loose of the true genius of personality. It's always captivating. There's no such thing as a boring person if they're being true to themselves. It's the same with your church! You can't say that the Rocky Mountains are more riveting than the outback of Australia. You can't say the Welsh valleys are more beautiful than the wetlands of Florida. Each is unique, each has a wonder, and each is captivating. Your personality is like that, as is the true personality of your church. It's captivating and increasingly attractive the truer you are to it. It's how God designed everyone to be. It's time to hoist up and revel in this unique attraction called "personality".

Alongside your personality, how much of your ministry is fashioned by fear itself? Sometimes we're afraid of really being ourselves for fear of losing either the elderly or the young. We fear "exclusivity".

The "lightweight" sanguine type personality tries to become a heavyweight intellectual to appease the more serious church member. The "teacher type" personality tries to become hip to reach the young people (it's never, ever hip to try to be hip!). It's right to do all we can to bring all the people with us and it's right to become "all things to all men", but that is a truth that should never be driven by fear. It fits only in the realm of sacrifice and love, adjustment and balance. Not fear. You've got to be yourself to lay it down. You can't give up what you don't possess.

3. The power of the sacred

We carry the legacy of centuries of religion. The great divide between the spiritual and the secular still rules today. Our list is complete: the spiritual includes prayer, gifts, the word of God, fellowship, communion . . . the secular includes work, watching TV, business opportunities, politics, and having a laugh. Our lives, however, are not divided into sacred and secular. There are only two categories: the sacred and the carnal. Either you're doing the will of the Father, or you're not. Money, prayer and personality are all gifts that can be used in both arenas. Both can be tools for a holy life, or tools for an unholy life. To "seek first His kingdom" is not advice that segregates the spiritual from the secular. It's a verse that segregates the eternal from the temporal. It also speaks of heavenly priorities. To "seek first His Kingdom" is not to leave our quest for finance filed under "s" for secular or "c" for carnal, but to dedicate and submit our quest to the building of His kingdom. Our personality is the same. It is to be dedicated to our quest to build the Kingdom. It's not secular, it's sacred.

4. The power of freedom

All of our personalities have been marred, suppressed and distorted by sin. Our redemption is not only of our spirits, but also of our minds, souls, and bodies (culminating in our resurrected form). Jesus died to redeem your soul. That's everything that makes you, you. His vision is to free your soul from inferiority, insecurity, insignificance, and insincerity, and restore you to the wholeness and fullness of the blueprint that God held for you before the world began. Be delivered today and allow the true colours of your God-given personality to radiate and impregnate the world around you. It's time to replace "grey" with iridescent purple, incandescent pink, subtle shades of turquoise and rich, earthy browns. You are magnificent.

Each of us and each of our churches represents the rich and diverse variety found in God's creation. Together we express the fullness of Christ. God's world on God's earth. No more imitation or impersonation. No more competition. In church life, and in life itself, you can't help but take on the characteristics of those you admire and spend time with. A son, however, is never a clone of his father. We will all be influenced by those we admire, but in the process let's never disown one of the greatest powers that we have in our possession – the power of originality. Let the divine *spark*.

I've found that a simple key to keeping excitement, character, and individuality alive and distinct in my church, is to advocate a simple rule: *Ban Beige!* Why is it that some people who used to paint the town red now spend their time painting their church beige? God hates beige. There's an enemy lurking around your back door and his name is "average". People who once excelled in their hedonistic lifestyles now sit pleasantly in the twentieth row, blending nicely into the background of church life. Whatever happened to them? What does salvation do to pizzazz? Those who once showed creative genius in different forms of stealing, robbing, lying and cheating, have now become good people – very good, but very, very boring people.

Strewn at the foot of the cross are not only the weeds and roots of sin, but also the fertile soil around which the roots entwined. Bits of personality, stones of creativity, and strands of ingenious family history lie abandoned. It's time to go back to the cross and take back the stuff we should never have jettisoned.

The spirit of religion is designed to keep us colour blind. Everything in life is black or beige. Religion majors on sacrifice, seriousness, and striving. It de-personalises and de-motivates; reducing everyone and everything to a backdrop of magnolia.

It's time to ban beige. Go on a beige watch. Make red, not beige. It's true that sparkle, passion and pizzazz need to be severed from the motivations that once drove their users to selfish gain, but it's our role to make sure that they're not left abandoned at the Jordan River of the Promised Land. We want them reconnected to a new heart, resulting in the mighty accelerations of the dreams of heaven. Pizzazz is our Christian heritage.

Here are some poignant expressions to live by . . .

- beige sky at night, devil's delight
- come out from the beiges of history or there'll be beige to pay
- get a clean beige of health
- don't ever visit beigeing (sorry!)
- stop being the beige sheep of the family
- catch someone beige handed

Whoever heard of Macy Beige, Beige Floyd, Cilla Beige or The Average Beige Band anyway?!

The leadership challenge

When enthusiastic people get saved they can become their own worst enemy. Their enthusiasm in hating sin and hating its penetration into their soul can result in both a hatred for sin and a hatred for who they were while they sinned. They fail to separate the gift (of being fearfully and wonderfully made) from the motivation (a deceptive heart) and ditch both at the foot of the cross. They then proceed to live a Christian life that's reduced to the realm of sacrifice and duty, adopting a personality and disposition that neither suits them nor agrees with them. Many eventually go on to have a Christian mid-life crisis. It's a crisis of personal identity, not positional identity. It's time for us to reconnect the sparkle of inner identity with their new identity that was won for them through the cross and resurrection.

How to not take yourself so seriously

Most leaders are too intense for the 21st Century. Don't get me wrong – they're very good – but so stodgy! Like a building with no windows, they personify fortress-like strength of convictions; but who wants to live in a place with no windows? To fill a wall with a window doesn't really weaken it – but it does make it more approachable, more hospitable, and much more attractive! Breezy, light-heartedness brings a 21st Century balance to the thick walls of unbending conviction.

In fact, it's one of the cornerstones of 21st Century culture: "Don't take yourself too seriously", coined with the catch phrase, "Lighten up!" As a minister, preacher, and leader, you can bridge the cultural divide using a catapult or a canon, but the best way is to build bridges of relationship, and that means you and I need to be entirely relatable!

"Relatability" is so difficult for people who see themselves as "watchmen on the walls". Being a "bastion of the truth" can wipe the smile off anyone's face. You can be too serious in your sincerity to hold onto what is good and what is right. We can even think that it all depends upon us. Responsibility is good, but being overly responsible will dampen all of the joy that seeks to rise from the heart and end up on the face!

When Jesus said, "My yoke is easy," He was declaring that "ease" was the true nature of Christian living. Can you believe it? In a recent survey of a zillion Christians, the question was put, "Do you find Christian living easy?" Our survey said a resounding, "You've got to be kidding!"

For most people, Christian living is far too difficult because they're always involved in things that are none of their business. Here's a little list of five things that are none of your business.

1. Trying to do what only God can do

Only God can do miracles! We can't do them! All we can do is believe and step out. Many Christians pray too little, but many also pray too much. There is a point where the pray-er leaves the prayer in the hands of the prayer-answering God and moves on.

2. Trying to work out how God will do what God said He will do

That's His business. Deuteronomy 29:29 says that the *"hidden things belong to God, but the revealed things belong to man."* We should walk in the light that we know of and trust Him in the darkness. Spurgeon once said, "He who believes what he knows shall soon know more clearly what he believes."

3. Worrying about tomorrow

Tomorrow is God's business. It's in a world of its own. It's our job to have faith and step out in obedience today. Life is about today. We have such a hard time being human that many Christians try to look and sound a bit more than human. Super-spirituality is a mask for insecurity. If we do the stuff the Bible tells us to do, it will be easier for God to do the stuff He's told Himself to do!

4. Prophesying the timing of God

Most of the time God reinforces His promises to us regarding His nature and His outcomes. He rarely tells us the timing and rarely gives us the full map to our destination. Most Christians give up because they invented, not the word of God, but the timings of God. The timings of God are held by the provenance of God. We expect, we anticipate ... and whenever He wants to, God acts.

5. Other people's decisions

The decisions that people make are none of our business. There's one thing that God will not do, even through our prayers, and that is circumnavigate people's decision-making ability (their free will). It's our job to influence, not invade. Even when we pray for people to be saved, God's answers generally come in the form of relighting people's conscience, giving them a more spacious and conducive environment in order to make a more clear-cut decision to accept or reject Him. You aren't responsible for the decisions made by your congregational members, or for decisions made by anyone outside of your church. You are responsible "to" your church and "to" the world around you. You are to "compel" them to come, but not "make" them come! It's time to stop trying to push people into various levels of commitment to Christ and it's time to simply present people with the opportunity to make ever-increasing commitments to Christ.

Rule Number 6

Recently in our in-house Megacentre publication for our church, I noticed a huge error in my article on "Faith, hope and love!" I assumed that everyone had been incredibly inspired by my scriptural reference. I quoted from the passage about Jonathan and his armour bearer which declares, "God will save by many or by few." I blame it on my handwriting (which is too much like a doctor's), but it had been translated in the typing: "God will save by money or by fear"! It wasn't even on the same continent! For a minute I was stunned. My temperature started to rise and then I remembered "Rule

Number 6". I was shown by the Spirit of God that it was all really, really funny – even for a perfectionist like me!

Rule Number 6 stands alone. There is no rule number 1, 2, 3, 4, 5 or 7. Here's a story about it taken from *The Art of Possibility* by Benjamin Zander:

> Two Prime Ministers are sitting in a room discussing affairs of state. Suddenly a man bursts in, apoplectic with fury, shouting and stamping and banging his fist on the desk. The resident Prime Minister admonishes him: "Peter," he says, "kindly remember Rule Number 6," whereupon Peter is instantly restored to complete calm, apologises and withdraws. The politicians return to their conversation, only to be interrupted, yet again, twenty minutes later, by an hysterical woman gesticulating wildly, her hair flying. Again the intruder is greeted with the words: "Marie, please remember Rule Number 6." Complete calm descends once more and she too withdraws with a bow and an apology. When the scene is repeated for a third time, the visiting Prime Minister addresses his colleague, "My dear friend, I've seen many things in my life, but never anything as remarkable as this. Would you be willing to share with me the secret of Rule Number 6?" "Very simple," replies the resident Prime Minister. "Rule Number 6 is, 'Don't take yourself so g-damn seriously.' "Ah," says his visitor, "That's a fine rule." After a moment of pondering, he inquires, "And what, may I ask, are the other rules?" "There aren't any."

I react when people say at the end of a time of worship, "Let's keep this spirit that we've entered into and not disturb it." The place then moves from inspired reflectiveness to inward morbidity. Human psychology cannot maintain solemnity for long periods except in certain, unusual, circumstances. To lighten the atmosphere is to keep everyone looking up and not down. I love "cutting in" on what people would see as "a flow", because in every meeting, many flows flow as one to produce multi-dimensional outcomes! To "lighten up" is to keep the flow! To stay too serious too long creates what the Australian aboriginals call a "billabong". It's part of a river that no longer flows!

You are a very funny person. British humour is the best in the world because (primarily outside of the church) they love to laugh at themselves. The Aussies laugh at others, Americans play with slapstick, but the British know how to display all of their eccentricities at the expense of themselves!

The best thing that a leader can do is get two or three young people to impersonate them and heartily laugh along at the light-hearted mockery! Far from disrespect, it's a steam releasing exercise. Just as comedians say stuff we all think, but wouldn't dare to say, a little parody goes a long way!

The way you walk is funny; the way you preach is funny; the way you put on that loving expression to cover up mental vacancy is funny. That high maintenance person that you really do love is funny too!

Just as every cloud has a silver lining (Hezekiah 3:2), every situation has a funny side. A big dollop of laughter is just what the doctor ordered for the 21st Century church . . . and it begins with you!

The spirit of cheekiness

Cheekiness is to have fun with social boundaries and to overstep certain parameters with a twinkle in your eye. Cheekiness is "naughty", but, in the words of Paul de Jong from Christian Life Centre in Auckland, naughty, but not "naughty naughty". With a short study of the life of Jesus it's easy to see that many

Christians are "nicer" than Jesus was, and it's also easy to see that many Christians are more "conservative" than Jesus ever was. It appears that Jesus was both compassionate and cheeky! How much is cheekiness a part of heaven? Let's find out!

1. The first miracle
Billions of years in the planning, the choice was made. The first miracle in the miracle ministry of Jesus Christ would not be the healing of a leper or a blind man . . . it would be the creation of wine! To immediately tread in an area that has created conflict throughout the Church for twenty-one centuries is highly controversial. Is Heaven a cheeky place? By all accounts that was not a traditional way to start a mission of compassion!

2. The "Pigs can Fly" saga
To cross a lake and deliver a "legion" of two thousand spirits is a mighty task full of power and compassion. To take a thriving pig breeding business and decimate it in one swoop is a strangely humorous scenario. That's "out of the box" living that breaks the nicer-than-nice view many have of Jesus.

3. The pop quiz
"Who do men say I am?" Jesus was either sincerely interested in the fact that some say He's Jeremiah (!) or He was entering into a serious proclamation with light-hearted banter.

4. The "mud in the eye" incident
Again, it's strange that Jesus didn't just say, "Be healed!" To spit, stir, spread and send away must certainly have deeper connotations. It must have been mildly amusing, watching a blind man with a mud pack heading to a distant pool.

5. The people watching

To hang around and see how much people are placing in the offering bowl would seem a little precocious for a group of disciples, yet out of a lazy Sunday afternoon comes a profound lesson: "This woman gave more than everyone else put together!" It's time for the Church to break free of the confines that keep it too serious to operate effectively in the 21st Century. It's imperative to hold deep conviction, but this must be accompanied by a spoonful of cheekiness in order to mirror the very nature of God Himself!

Essential leadership kit (to enjoying the journey)

- Exercise the power of originality. Stop copying from other people and find ways of truly expressing what you truly believe.
- Stop taking yourself so seriously!
- Stop trying to do what only God can do. It's time to stop striving and enjoy the journey.
- Take away the dividing line between the secular and the spiritual and banish the spirit of religion from your life and the lives of the people you lead (and don't get too serious doing it!)
- It's time to get cheeky!

The Diary Archives

3rd May 2000

It's been a really intense time! The last month has been taken up with reinventing the church for the start of the new year in September. It's been a real challenge. Dave and Anne are off to Hungary and there has been a necessity to really cut expenses and reinvent the budget. I'm releasing my schools' worker into youth evangelism across the nation and I'm bringing down the number of people who mill around the church centre during the day. I've realised that there is a tipping point when it comes to the number of people working in the centre and overall work inefficiency. Most people would think that the more people are working, the more gets done. What tends to happen is that overall administration becomes inefficient with so many separate administrative centres being formed, socialising increases with the need to say hello to so many people, and vision sharpness tends to decrease. Without cutting right back, I believe that there is an optimum functional level.

It's been a real challenge taking back the control of things and changing from delegated leadership back to directive leadership. With God's amazing help I think I'm dealing with it all. There have been so many undercurrents of emotion. I've had to give the church over to the Lord so many times lately. I've had to be strong and loving. It's brought back a lot of memories from the last time I did this. Things weren't good and everything hit the fan. Leaders refused to relinquish their leadership and a number rebelled. I've had to face it and I know that that's the past, not the future. I'm sure that God's enlarged me since and increased the size of my heart. I have a personality type, though, that when I get a new pair of shoes, I never wear the old ones again. My new shirts totally replace old ones. I will always have to watch my pragmatic side in the launching of "new things". I've done that with people in the past, only to provoke feelings of rejection. I've dismissed the old for the new too quickly. I am now so aware that this isn't just about brand new corporate vision, but a progressive vision for every individual. With my personality I also find that nothing has sentimental value. I can change friendships easily and be quite rootless! There's always a voice nudging me to move house and move city! I'm resisting it. I am aware that it's also a part of having moved so often since

I was born. As a family we never developed close relationships and have been quite independent in all of the locations we've lived in. It's taken the Lord a lot of work to develop a shepherd's heart within me that is committed to the pasture He has given. I can really understand it (but I don't really like it) when certain leaders say of themselves that they're the visionaries of the church and distance themselves from the overall shepherding of the church. I really believe that the senior leader's ministry is the shepherding ministry and being a visionary is actually a part of being a shepherd.

From last October to last month we've had a 15% drop in church attendance. That's a 15% drop in seven months. I think that's been reflected in the drop in our finances. We deal with so many people who suffer from what I have had to deal with – rootlessness and restlessness. It's our challenge to create roots beneath them. This month, however, our attendance is picking up again. I know that when you begin building projects you can often lose people because of the increased demands, especially upon their pockets. Where your treasure is your heart is also! Right now, I really want to increase the sense of family amongst us and increase an environment that is conducive to establishing stronger relationships.

Jenny and I went to an "all paid for" marriage retreat last week. At night it turned into a prophecy session! The pastor prophesied that I needed to lighten up! I realise that there's a "boy" side to my personality that many people rarely see. The pastor also prophesied that I would come into a new style of preaching – more relaxed and humorous. He declared we would have a national influence and openings with the media. Jenny had a great word about being the Marilyn Hickey of the UK! She doesn't really know who Marilyn Hickey is, but it sounds powerful!

It was funny to see one of the couples who had done a lot of damage to our church and then left to create their own church in attendance at the retreat. It was a litmus test for me to see how much God had done in me since that time. We had a good chat and I felt free and easy. Praise God!

Today's update:
The releasing of our youth worker was the right decision, but the transition was not successfully accomplished. He felt called to another church and because we refused to affirm the call, the parting wasn't amicable.

8th June 2000
It's been a month of coming back to directive leadership. I don't like it because I want everyone to be happy! I've taken back the reigns of so much of what I had previously delegated. It's been a struggle! I find it so hard to relinquish control. I so want **team** and not just a collection of different visions. The first step must be to give the clear sounds of captaincy. I want to streamline the church – make it leaner and fitter for the next move and to take it to the next level.

I have been the recent target of criticism! People don't like change and there have been times lately when people's bad agendas and sharp insecurities have risen to the surface. I so want people to simply love God, become like God, and love people. So many people love it when I focus on them and when I spend time with them, but the moment my attention goes else-where, they collapse. Lord, give them a revelation of Yourself. I'm confident, though, that we're designing for the next level and not just pandering to the present. We'll win. I believe that God has taken Jenny and me to the next level and we are to take our church on to that level.

On a lighter note, I just borrowed a bike and cycled 330 miles right across Ireland and across Wales in five days (in fact, if you take out a day in Dublin, you could say four days!). I love cycling. I really need to buy a bicycle. I went with some guys from church and had a brilliant time. On a personal note, my dad is very sick. He's seventy-seven years old and needs a heart operation, but he's too weak to have one just yet. Also, my brother's family (in America) have just left him – too much tension for far too long. I see my dad once a year in Sydney while attending the Hillsong Conference. We meet, chat, have lunch and then plan to meet the following year! I haven't seen my brother for five years or so. It's quite a difficult relationship. I enjoy seeing him, but he's pretty reactive. We are, what you'd call, a dysfunctional family! I feel for my mum as her whole life has been invested into my dad. They divorced many years ago, but still see each other often and dad regularly stays for a week in every month. (He lives in Sydney and mum lives in Canberra. He spends the rest of the time writing books – mostly dictionaries!) They've become more and more dependent over the years. We need a breakthrough from God.

15th June 2000

I told my leadership class that the stuff that was in the room – a sense of family, commitment, vitality, faith, loyalty, perseverance and diligence – is the stuff of revival. It carries with it the massive force of heaven that defeats all spiritual powers. I think it really empowered them.

Jenny's first "Fabulous You" women's conference is beginning today. There has been an incredible sense of unity amongst the women in the putting on of the conference. I believe the unity is as powerful as the ministry itself.

In the light of the reinvention of our church and the introduction of some new key players I have had two couples recently say they're leaving. I could see it coming, but hoped that they would make the changes to stay. Deep down, I know that they've never really been a part. They've never really laid down their agenda (or their ministry franchise). They feel like they don't belong and have secretly noted that the emergence of a new breed of leaders arising is the closing of the door to the possibility of their public emergence in the near future. It's similar to a time a number of years ago when we had another upsurge of new leaders. The older "would be's" (who tended to be in their fifties) reacted and many left. There's a sense of loss in my heart that they failed to make the changes necessary to come with us, but there's also a relief that they've quit contesting things behind the scenes! I'm concerned, though, over all of the people they personally influence in the life of the church. I've got to realise, however, it's God who builds His Church. I'm confident that we're entering a season of growth that will surprise all of us. I believe that we're building a church that will be more incredible with each year that passes. Our people are committed, have a huge heart for new people, and are hungry for impact.

Leadership Leads,
Management Doesn't

Don't give an order, create a culture

Leadership Leads, Management Doesn't

The Confusion of Church Life

In your church there is a culture at work whether you believe it or not. Its force is staggering and the results are predictable. People are a product of their environment. Why do showbiz stars often have celebrity parents? Robbie Williams' dad is also an entertainer. Lee Evans' dad was a comedian. Shania Twain's mum was a singer. The answer? Culture. Great churches have great cultures created by great leaders.

In this chapter we're going to look at how to create a culture that establishes all that you want to see happen – the difference between leadership, management, grass roots ministry, and some of the wrong thinking that many leaders accept without challenging.

Don't give an order, create a culture

Culture determines what grows and what doesn't. Creating a hothouse environment will cause Amazonic growth, while creating an ice house will cause Arctic growth. A cynical environment engenders cynics and a diligent environment ensures diligence. If culture plays such a powerful role in shaping people's lives, we need to create a culture in our churches that produces the results that we really want, rather than the results we put up with.

Many leaders are primarily involved with eliminating fires rather than creating them. Fires of controversy and conflict abound, yet fires of enthusiasm and sacrifice remain un-kindled. Many leaders allow other people to determine their church's culture. Dominant people with self-seeking motives create cultures of inferiority and supremacy. Unconfident leaders create people unwilling to commit to any major initiative. It's essential that every leader becomes a "controlling" leader and controls the culture behind every activity that's performed.

Here are some ways to create a champion church culture that creates a champion church:

1. Promote all of the right people

It's essential that the right people are lifted up, on public display, admired and revered to all. Exhibit what you want your church to become. Putting the right people in all the right places does wonders in changing the atmosphere. There are many people who exhibit the attitude and disposition I want everyone to have. There are people whose "excellent" spirit is the future of the entire church. I will only involve people with a heart of faith and a passion for the house of God to demonstrate that to others in the house of God.

You need to place the right people on the welcome team, on announcements, on the testimonials, and on the tech team. In many churches, valuable time is taken up by ardent prayers and prophesiers who do not hold the heart you want to foster. Sound desks are notorious for harbouring a different spirit from that being engendered from the front of a church that's building a powerful culture. It's time to fill up service time with involvement from the best DNA carriers while squeezing out all other life forms.

In our church we regularly give gifts and awards to people who have done well and to unsung heroes. We deliberately exalt the humble to create a culture filled with humility. Those demanding recognition never get it. They're always pipped to the post by the lowly.

What you tolerate you will not change. It's time to bring certain people to the end of a "season" of conscious stagnation and move in the living radiators of the desired culture.

2. Build the right team

It's always difficult to challenge bad attitudes and it's impossible to challenge pride directly as pride makes the wearer deny that they were to blame. The best way to change a team is to increase the number of people who live in the culture you want to promote. Often they're your true "sons" in the faith. The sheer momentum of the new culture will clash with the now lesser momentum of the old. Issues are no longer debated on an even match. The old ways move aside to adhere to the new culture.

3. Create a partnership programme

Bring all of today's programmes to a conclusion, except for the ones that you and your team are directly at the helm of. Create a partnership class that creates partners in the vision, rather than members of the church. Teach the true values of the early Church, the true purpose of the early Church, and the new expectations you're going to work with from now on! If we are the Body of Christ, if He died for the Church, and if we are Christ's ambassadors, we need to walk worthy of the calling. This has to mean an end to lateness, an increase in regular attendance, growing of tithes and generous offerings, involvement in a department, and quick conflict resolution. If people want to rise to being partners, let them agree to the five or so expectations of effective partnership. It raises the game. It puts an end to the old and marks the beginning of the new.

4. Create a personal culture that's indestructible

We are not primarily preachers, but living epistles, read by all. Our lives play out all of our beliefs. People become what we are in private, not what we profess in public. It's essential for leaders to create a private culture that encourages all of Christ's attributes in increasing measure. The church's primary leader needs to set the example in every core value. You can't just pray occasionally, yet expect a praying church, even with a regular intercessors group. It's the role of leaders to intercede. You can't have a faith-filled church if your private world is filled with cynicism and doubt. Every leader must walk worthy of the calling and pave the way.

5. Do sermon series

One of my congregation was shocked that I should preach on enthusiasm and see so few turn out for the night meeting. I told him to hold on – people rarely change because of one sermon. Guest speakers rarely impact churches. Progressive, unrelenting preaching of a word from God creates a culture that gradually creates the desired outcome. People often say that God has spoken to them and the scripture or truth they declare is the same as that preached in the series – the one before the last. They don't even realise that, but ownership of the truth makes its authorship irrelevant!

6. Celebrate the small victories

London is a city filled with monuments. Our churches shouldn't be transfixed with monuments to the past; rather we should be creating new ones from today's successful people. David's mighty men slew giants because they were raised in a giant slaying culture. David slew a giant first because he was raised in a bear and lion slaying culture. He celebrated smaller victories that led to greater victories. Don't despise the day of small beginnings. Acceleration is more important than velocity and momentum is more important than size. If things are taking off, celebrate every act and every encounter associated with it. It will create!

7. Don't keep up with the Jones'

It's better to have a worship team without a drummer than use a drummer who lives by his own agenda. It's better to have no team than a bad team. Some have said recently that people need a sense of belonging before they take on a sense of believing. I don't believe it. People who have no faith in my church never get a true sense of belonging. It's essential that I don't create a surrogate sense of belonging through encouraging participation and ignoring culture. Church is first and foremost about discipleship. From that discipleship flows true faith in Christ. Let that be the guiding core value of our church culture. When a culture is created and nurtured, so many of the things that once caused you to bang your head against the wall no longer occur. Peer pressure takes precedence. Latecomers are a minority. Miserable people stand out a mile. Flashy people don't seem to fit in any more to the fabric of the church. New converts succeed more readily and excel more steadily as they draw on the nutrients that are in the soil of the church. Attitude checks are done by the fourth rank of leadership, not always by the first rank. Everyone knows what's wanted and what's expected. Everyone pulls their weight. Spearheading and tweaking become the domain of core leadership. Fire fighting becomes a thing of the past.

8. Eliminate excuse mentality

One of the great resistances to creating great teams that create great churches is the development of a culture of excuse making!

Almost everyone has an excuse for not achieving destiny. In John 5:6, Jesus asks an invalid, *"Do you want to get well?"* His excuse that someone else always gets into the pool for healing before he does demonstrated his loss of the passion that could have led to his healing. He no longer sat, ready and waiting, on the edge of the pool. Excuses abound in every church, team, and individual. Part of the art of leadership is to encourage personal responsibility and kill the culture of excuse making at every turn.

It amazes me how difficult it has been in the past to find the reason why certain things weren't done by the required deadline in our church. The department leader, when asked about it, would cast the blame on the team member who failed to complete the task. The team member would then blame the mechanic who wasn't able to get his car back to him in time. The mechanic obviously had a good excuse, but the end result was that no one took final responsibility.

It's essential in church life that leaders delegate and do not abdicate. To delegate is to get others to assist you in the accomplishment of the task at hand. To abdicate is to pass the task, and its responsibility, to someone else.

Leadership takes it on the chin. I have told my team that if it looks like we're going to miss a deadline, to let me know beforehand so we can find other means to make it happen in time, or, so that we can create another deadline. It also means that the leader is carefully monitoring the project in its final stages. While it's good to empower others, the responsibility still lies with the one who did the empowering.

In my book, *The Top Ten of Everything About Christian Leadership*[1] I outline the top ten excuses used by people to escape responsibility when a leader gives them a task to complete. Here's that top ten with each of the excuses expanded upon.

▶ **1. *I'll pray about it*.** Prayer is often a scapegoat for direct action. "I'll pray about it" is either the truth, a big fat lie to palm you off, or a form of super spirituality where the seeker is waiting for an angel to appear on the number 42 bus. Many people don't realise the capacity they could actually have if they simply took responsibility and challenged their laid-back nature. Busyness is a huge weapon in the hand of a saint. If they just organised it they'd be surprised at how much time they really did have to do what was asked of them. No more hiding behind prayer!

▶ **2. *I've been led by the Spirit to another ministry*.** Often we sanction people "being led" when what they really needed was to "be refreshed". People "feel led" more often through boredom than via the Holy Spirit. We sometimes make a huge mistake by giving someone who's bored with their job, greater responsibility in an effort to kick start their inner engine. Their problem is that their eyes have dimmed and vision no longer drives them. It's a job. That's all. In our church we don't do jobs, we fulfil vision. Where vision abounds there's no time to ever get bored or be "led by the Spirit". Don't make up jobs for bored people. They need an eye appointment, not another plate to spin. They need refreshing – not repositioning.

▶ **3. *I need time out*.** "Time out" is usually "pull out". It should only be used in emergency situations. If it's "time out" with God, how long can you spend on the couch

with God? I find that after two hours or so I'm ready
to get going. I've learnt that after recharging on the
mountain, it's time to take it to the valleys. Even
with mountain top experiences, the majority of our
sustenance from God comes from "takeaways". God's
"takeaways" are found in abundance along the road. Isaiah
49:9 tells us, *"They will feed beside the roads and find pasture
on every barren hill."* Time out can also be an excuse for
"a little folding of the arms". Busyness isn't a curse. It's an
asset. Stopping and starting can easily break the power of
momentum and cause life to be more difficult than it was
designed to be. People need to stop cutting the pace and
start running consistently into the purposes of God.

▶ **4. My gifts don't lie in that particular area.** I recently
pulled up at some traffic lights and became conscious of
how fantastic I was feeling. After a quick self-analysis I
discovered the reason for my feelings was because some of
my specific gifts were really being used, and as such, were
really making a difference. Why didn't I feel this way all of
the time? Answer – because much of what I do is done as a
generalist, not a specialist. Life is like that. You can't afford
to be too defined. It's all hands on deck with all of our
energies flowing out of the gift of love and our love for life
itself. To be too "gift focused" is to entertain self-absorption
as well as limit God's ability to create character within us.

▶ **5. My ministry is more prophetic than practical.** I once had
some "prophets" in my church tell me about a coming
move of the Spirit sweeping children into its wake from
Lands End to John O'Groats. After calling for children's
workers to respond to our current needs, not one of these
people signed up. End of story.

▶ **6. *I'll do it when God moves me*.** It's all so wrong. God
says **"Yes"**, until He says **"No"**. Let the peace of God be
the umpire of your heart (Colossians 3:15). The umpire is
not there to provide motivation or movement to the
game, but rather to tell you when to stop when you've
gone over the mark. It's "all systems go" unless God
says, "all systems stop." I never got a word from God to
build a children's centre – I just never heard God say
"stop". My ear is always open to hearing the "whistle"
of the umpire and until I do there's so much to get
on with.

▶ **7. *My time is all taken up with intercession*.** There is no
ministry gift of "intercession" in the New Testament.
There is no office of "intercessor". You can pray and
intercede, but you can't repent on behalf of, take
responsibility for, or carry the sins of, anyone else but
yourself. Only Jesus can fully intercede. We are priests,
but He is the only High Priest. I have found that a large
majority of people who claim the gift of intercession are
very insecure people. They are searching for significance.
The feeling of being "ordinary" is too overwhelming for
them and yet, either through a lack of personal revelation,
or a lack of opportunities to serve, they find themselves
caught in the spirit of the world.

▶ **8. *I've come to the end of a season*.** You usually mark the
end of a season by the coming on of a new season. Don't
allow people to be caught "seasonless". (In my church if
someone wants to resign from ministry because they feel
like it's the end of a season, we do let them go straight
away). Commitment is the child of vision and if both have
died, it's better that they leave now. It's always better to

play a team of nine than to be always tripped up by two feet-draggers in a team of eleven.

▶ **9. *Just don't turn up*.** Excuses, excuses, excuses! There are always too many to be true. It's time to eliminate excuse mentality. Some time ago I went on a mission to eradicate the vermin of excuses with my staff! If we blame someone else and they blame the wife who blames her dad who blames the government – you're stuck. A great church is one that's "unstuck" and taking personal responsibility for all of its actions.

▶ **10. *I'm leaving church. They're all a bunch of hypocrites*.** They say that if you find a perfect church, don't join it – you'll mess it up! People who leave church often never arrived. They were pot plants, not house plants. Don't give a pastoral role to someone who is only a servant of the house. Only give pastoral positions to people who are sons of the house. Servants do a job, sons do life. Servants do their duty, sons live for the future. Servants leave, sons stay. Build on sonship.

Old wisdom verses new

They say that leaders are readers. I believe that leaders ought to be thinkers. There are a numbers of assumptions that need to be confronted in the life of leadership in order to lift the lid on leadership and see a new way of thinking and living arise. Here's a list of assumptions worth challenging:

Old wisdom number 1:

What we need is not equal giving, it's equal sacrifice
If I get another letter suggesting that if each church member

gave £5 or $5 a month then we'd have more than enough to complete our noble mission (yes, that mission of incredible value that is currently wilting because of your stinginess and greed), I know exactly where to file it. It's the last gasp of leadership that fails to understand the nature of follower-ship. The plan will fail, the project will hobble along, and cynicism within the local church will grow another membrane.

The problem with grovel letters is that they smack of grovelling! That is no way to run an organisation. The lowest form of leadership is the call for communistic commitment. Vision should "runneth over". The power of inspiration takes people far beyond the call of duty. If you want a few lousy fivers to come through the mailbox each month to provide for your vision, persist at your own peril.

Another problem is the insipidness of a fiver a month. That's £1.25 a week. That's nothing! And that's the problem. The true colours of the magnificence of the project have now been watered down to the colour of nothing. All leaders gather round and listen ... no one likes nothing. Nothing has never inspired no one! If you're going to start making cheap cars then take the Mercedes badge off and replace it with another brand name. If you have a noble task don't pitch for un-noble hand outs. Sure, I understand that a fiver a month can raise sixty a year. It soon adds up. You and I might understand that, but the potential donator rarely does. It's "buy in on the cheap". Nobody likes that so few people do it.

The greatest error in it all is to attempt to break the 80/20 rule. This magnificent rule states that 80% of the giving comes from 20% of the people. It's a rule that annoys a lot of people. It appears to reek of unfairness and is challenged by desperate mathematical visionaries who think that if it can be broken we'll have multiplied resources for the kingdom's coffers.

Establishing the giving principle

Leaders, pioneers, "pastorpreneurs", preachers and apostles –
read my lips: The 80/20 rule is here to stay. Save your
ammunition for a conquest that can be won. The reason that
it's here to stay is because you make it so (or you ought to!).
The Kingdom is not built on equal giving, we all know that. But
it's not based upon equal sacrifice either. The degree of sacrifice
that leaders offer is higher than the degree of sacrifice of non-
leaders. That's what makes leaders "leaders". If it were not so,
the leader would eventually be replaced by those non-leaders
who are actually leading.

It's leadership that creates the 80/20 rule. They insist on
sacrificing more than the masses. They make the "giving
profile" lopsided. Let's do the maths: every healthy church is
made up of three groupings of people. Firstly we have the
"outer third". This is the social set, as well as the sincerely
inquisitive. Next we have the "middle third" which contains
those genuinely on a journey of follower-ship. Lastly we have
the "inner third" who are the initiators and the engine room of
church life. The giving is already skewed. 66% of the giving is
done by 33% of the people. But within the inner third are the
core leaders who make up one third of that third. We've now
buckled the profile of giving even further. 80% of the giving is
done by 20% of the people.

Breaking the golden rule

It's a bad thing for a church or a growing organisation to ever
break that rule. Wherever it has been broken, one of two things
has happened. Firstly, they've lost their fringe. Your fringe is
your future. Because everyone is on a journey it's unhealthy to
have a homogeneous group of "full on" saints. When leaders
say that they've got 90% of the people involved in some form of
ministry I quake. It sounds like the church has lost its

evangelistic edge that always creates a "healthy" fringe. A healthy fringe is a place where people can hide from commitment and issues as they make up their mind about you and God. Fair play!

Secondly, they've lost their leadership edge. Your leaders are leading the cause of Christ and the vision that carries it. They ought to be the first to give every time. They ought to reach deeper into their pockets than anyone else. Their example becomes an inspiration to everyone who's following.

Proverbs tells us that the heart is the wellspring of life (Proverbs 4:23). Out of the heart of your church, which is its leadership, shall flow the streams that whet the appetite of all who follow. If the heart is good then goodness will eventually follow. (80/20 is restored, but both the 80 and the 20 are far fuller than ever before).

Raising your game

Never let leaders off the hook. You can't allow someone to lead in teaching or to lead a small group and yet be segregated from the overall life of the church. They must lead the corporate gathering, not just their own area of interest. Also, never let yourself off the hook. If you're a part of the core team, you must lead by example. Your level of giving should raise itself time and time again. That always unblocks the wells that, in turn, cause rivers of generosity to begin to flow.

Here are ten bullet points that can assist you in taking maximum advantage of the amazing 80/20 principle.

- Make it an honour and a rich privilege to be offered a partnership in the outworking of your incredible vision. Never cheapen it or make it cost nothing.
- Supply different partnership categories for giving. Let the highest category be really high. Call each category by an

inspiring name and let people be provoked to new levels of giving.

- Get the leaders to give first. Make sure you've cracked the back of the provision for the vision simply through the leaders alone.
- Always give by example. You may not say how much you're giving, but you can say what you've done to enable you to give so generously.
- Use the word "sacrifice" sparingly. To serve God is the best thing in the world. Make everything a delight, not a chore.
- Don't berate the non-givers – ignore them. Non-givers have plenty of other heart issues that make non-giving only one of their problems. Keep speaking life until the penny drops.
- Don't ever grovel – turkeys grovel, eagles fly. You're hungry for a positive outcome, but not overly desperate, because your ultimate faith is in God, not people.
- Always look for key national partners (if you're involved in a national vision.) Far more success comes from the giving of four large backers than cheap attempts to enrol 400 backers.
- Don't make a god out of goals. Both volunteer labour and miracle provision can constantly change the goalposts. Don't get caught out by fixing your goals in concrete.
- Stop trying to be a superhero – 80/20 is here to stay.

Old wisdom number 2:
People aren't rejecting God, they're just rejecting the container that God comes in
They say that it's not God that people have a problem with, it's

the Church. Because people are presented with a Church that's out of touch, marginalised, out of reach, and full of hypocrites, we are told that that's why people don't go to Church anymore. The Church has no attraction to them and therefore people are leaving (or not coming) in their droves.

If that is true, the opposite must then be true: if the Church is trendy, approachable, friendly, relevant, within reach, and filled with people who actually do what they believe, then people will come flooding back to Church, because it's not God that they have been rejecting. Even though there is an element of truth in this "old wisdom", I have found two things far more overwhelmingly true. Firstly, in leading a really contemporary Church, people still haven't flocked to us in droves. Personally, I have not found people knocking on my door in high numbers because I wear "Top Man" clothes and I'm really friendly, relevant and anointed! Secondly, when I got saved through the influence of friends who were committed Christians, I attended churches that were vastly different from the "pop" culture that I was used to. But my revelation overlooked the cultural disparity.

The truth that supersedes "presentation and packaging" is that the answer to reaping the harvest that Jesus told us about is not so much to do with "church style" as it is individual faith and the desire to search out and connect with the harvest and see it successfully reaped. The growing hunger of the lost will cause them to open their hearts to yours and those who go after the harvest will see God do great things.

People will rarely just come into a church meeting because they've heard that it's "hip"! Nothing will ever replace the power of faith, prayer, generosity, friendships and the gentle presentation of the gospel through life and testimony. The gospel remains the power of God that causes people to shift from darkness to light.

Old wisdom number 3:

When your church building is over 80% full, the church will automatically stop growing

They say that the size of your hall will put a cap on the number of people attending your congregation. Many statistics suggest that soon after a new, bigger facility is opened, the congregation begins to grow again.

Even though it is often true that to "go large" ushers in a larger congregation, the reason for it is not the reason given. Often the completion of a larger venue is the manifestation of the fulfilment of a word of faith. It's the action attached to the faith that precipitated a spiritual manifestation – the growth of the congregation. Alongside the results of faith are also the results of proven ministry. Paul told Timothy to entrust truth to "reliable men" who would, in turn, do likewise. Proven reliability is not just a biblical mandate that works downwards, but also upwards. People ought to follow ministry that proves itself through its actions and its fruitfulness. The larger facility often indicates the proof of great teamwork, great faithfulness, great generosity, and great favour from God. Many people then choose to entrust their lives to such a ministry.

There is no such thing as a cap at 80% full. If faith is abounding and all systems are go, the church will continue to outgrow the hall. New wisdom, though, moves to double services or to a larger facility before this ever takes place.

Old wisdom number 4:

People aren't looking for superstars

They say that the age of the superstar Christian leader is behind us and now is the time for authentic team building with leaders who blend into the fabric of their teams. They say that there are inherent dangers in putting your hope in one man and inherent dangers along the pathway of any leader who stands out from the rest. Stardom is a thing of the past and there's a lot of damage to show for it.

This is a classic case of throwing the baby out with the bath water. Paul told people to follow him. He set himself up on a pedestal for others to be inspired by and to imitate. The crucial difference between Paul and Robbie Williams is that Paul added, "*. . . as I follow Christ.*"

People are in desperate need of more heroes of the faith. In an age where very few Christian leaders stand out from the pack (leading to some "off the wall" type Christianity), the answer isn't, "no superstars please" but, "please give us more". Every mountain climber needs a Hillary to look up to and every long-distance runner needs a Bannister to be inspired by. Every Christian needs to be inspired by leaders who step out into unknown territory and come back with the spoils of war.

It is the devil's aim to discourage church organisations by starving them of inspiration, because inspiration will always result in increased motivation. While an unmotivated team is pointless, a motivated team is invincible.

We need both great teams and great individuals who will inspire us to climb the high peaks and endure the deep valleys. This is the day for multitudes of superstars to blaze a trail of glory to the King.

Old wisdom number 5:

There should be no barriers between the clergy and the laity
Ancient wisdom built pulpits that rose twenty feet above the people to give a clear demarcation between the priest and the pew gatherers. Ministers were told to have little to do with the people and to keep well away from forming friend-ships with the laity.

Old wisdom, which in the past three decades has swept away this ancient wisdom, tells us to get close to the people and make sure that you're accessible, vulnerable, and always available for the people (except at meal times). New wisdom says that if you want to have burnout and be regularly abused and abandoned, then stay with the old wisdom. Jesus spent most of His time with twelve men. Out of the twelve, he had three closest, and out of the three, he had one that was most special. Jesus defied political correctness. Not only were the twelve seemingly selected from one particular area, they were mostly young. It can't be right! There were times He opened up His "home" to the crowds and times when He moved away from the crowds.

New wisdom says that it's important not to intimately share your life with everyone outside of the pulpit. Not only are pearls often cast before "swine", but people so easily mistake the minister's warmth and accessibility as a promise that he'll be their best friend forever. The greatest mistake leaders make is to form close relationships with all the wrong people – people who think they have the ability to run alongside the leader, but who ultimately cannot sustain the pace for a lengthened period of time and ultimately drop out. Both parties can ultimately fail to deliver what the relationship initially promised, eventually leading to a degeneration of the friendship.

The problem with many churches isn't that they splinter or split. The problem lies in the initial formation of the relationships and friendships. Many should never have been formed. In our society, marriage breakdown is not the number one social problem: the problem is marriage creation. Many couples simply should never have got married. Many relationships are formed on the basis of personal insecurities. Often, this is the case in church life too. Teams are established because of the leader's insecurities. The fear of being seen as "dictatorial" leads many leaders to let go of their responsibilities and delegate to people who are unproven, unknown, and unaccountable. This will always lead to splintering. A revelation of the love of

God and the call of God is always at the root of excellent leadership.

It is essential that leaders take control of the relationships they develop using discernment and wisdom, knowing what limits to place on each level of intimacy. Leaders should be secure enough to both win new friends and influence people, as well as lose old friends and infuriate people!

Old wisdom number 6:

God alone shall supply all of our needs

Many forward thinking Christians are still caught in what I call a "wilderness mentality". They're expecting to find a money tree that will miraculously solve all of their provisional problems. They dream big and then look for a big God to fill in the blanks and "give" them "that building" or "that plot of land".

Many of the miracles that are publicly testified to in church life are wilderness miracles. Shoes that never wear out, food that simply arrives at the door, and unusual signs in the heavenlies, are all things for which we give God glory, but is it the high ground of the miraculous, or simply the nursery slopes of the miraculous, that God has in store for our lives? As church leaders do we go for the glamour and romance of the spectacular in the wilderness over the slightly more subdued, but just as potent, miracles of Canaan? Which gets the most publicity? Biblically, the wilderness was on the way to Canaan. It was never meant to be seen as a destination.

It always amazes us how good God is to new Christians. As babes in Christ, "miracles" seem to abound, but then seemingly "tail off" as they mature in Christ. Is it, though, a tailing off, or a transition to a different kind of miracle that has less gloss, but just as much substance? There are some crucial differences between the miracles of the wilderness and the miracles of Canaan. By understanding them we can help create and mould a church life that leads people to maturity without losing the "wow factor" of living for Jesus.

Wilderness miracles are subsistence miracles. Canaan miracles are abundance miracles. In the wilderness one pair of shoes was miraculously renewed. In Canaan, a land flowing with milk and honey, they had as many pairs of shoes as they were willing and able to create. Wilderness miracles require no planting. Canaan miracles require planting. Wilderness miracles are largely providential – they rely on the faith of the great leader and the prayers of others, rather than on personal believing. Canaan miracles are largely partnership dependent – the harvest you reap is in proportion to your sown seed. Understanding this can make a crucial paradigm shift in the thinking of our people.

Jesus didn't tell us to pray for the harvest, but to send labourers *into* the harvest. His focus was on *partnership*. Things rarely happen just through prayer unless you are a new Christian. Canaan miracles need a seed. Romans 8 tells us that faith comes by hearing and hearing comes from someone speaking. Someone speaking comes from someone going. I believe in prayer, but dismiss the emergence of the cult of prayer. Paul didn't stop writing a second letter to the Corinthian church because he was trusting God for the needs of the Jerusalem church. Jerusalem needed a miracle and Paul was convinced that the Corinthians would play a vital part in it. God rarely does creative miracles in the area of provision. Even though He could cause money to grow on trees or create a million pounds and place it in a briefcase just outside your front door, He rarely does it. Why? Because the greater kind of miracle in God's "cache" is the miracle of a changed heart. It's a creative miracle of a different kind: God changing the motivation of the heart and making someone become the source of someone else's supply.

For Christians, the Canaan miracle of people responding to others, and people connecting with others in order to respond to them, may be less dramatic than money falling out of the sky, but in reality it's just as powerful, because the hand of God lies behind it. Much of the Christian life is a "stitch up" between seed and harvest, a giver and receiver, prayer and responder. At the start of both Elijah's and Elisha's ministry they had an encounter with a solitary woman in need. The first had a little oil and a little flour and the second only had a little oil. The first woman gave what she had away and for the rest of her life was rewarded with an endless supply. The second woman obtained as many vessels as she could and was given as much return of oil as the number of vessels could hold. For the first woman, it was according to Elijah's word. For the second woman, it was according to her pots. That's Canaan living.

It's always a secret dream that a millionaire will walk into our churches and become a major financier of our visions. Far fewer people dream of creating millionaires. We have taken the scripture, "Seek first His kingdom" out of context. To seek God's kingdom is to seek after both the vision and provision of His kingdom, rather than simply seeking after "spiritual things" and putting our personal needs last. Just as it is important in church life to train and raise up workers for children's ministry, it is equally important to train and raise up those who will become vessels of provision which God will use to generate financial provision for His Kingdom. That is the difference between wilderness thinking (simply to be the beneficiary of a secret will) and Canaan living, which seeks to increase the wealth of ordinary people who will be used by God for His future purposes. Our generosity opens the windows of heaven, not just to the rare finds of riches, but also to the opportunity to create wealth through business investment, promotion, and the general favour of God.

Let's create churches where people are believing and working hard, acting in faith, and sowing seeds. Let's live in awe of the mystery of God, but at the same time demystifying the process through which God builds His Kingdom.

Get excited about the testimonies of the box of food on the doorstep and begin to magnify the great testimony of the businessman who, in obedience to faith, set up a distribution centre on the other side of town and saw his profits double. It's a miracle worth celebrating and will lift our churches from subsistence into abundance.

Essential leadership kit
(for smart thinking on the journey)

- Be a cultural architect, not a commander in chief.
- Know what you're up to – is it leadership, management, or grass roots ministry?
- Become a thinker – it's not equal giving or equal sacrifice ... it's not right to let everyone into your life ... and miracles never just fall out of the sky.

The Diary Archives

21st July 2000
I feel like I'm under immense pressure. Financially, we're still out in the deepest of water. Our main account is constantly being rescued by borrowing other monies outside of our tithes and offerings. Our building fund is nothing like it should be. There's no further interest in people leasing part of our property and a "millionaire" lead has only retrieved a token offering. Lord, help! We've had around ten earners leave the church, seriously affecting our financial stability. Besides all this, the Megacentre needs cleaning and all our interns have finished for the year!

I also feel that I can't muster up the energy to put on any more events or to have any guests visit us.

I have, however, enjoyed being with friends. I've got a new theme: "Enjoy the journey". I'm pretty exhausted by forced relationships. I know that the placing of some of my friends in leadership positions has been the straw that's caused a number of people to leave, but I can't keep on pursuing relationships that never seem to actually click together. In actual fact, I feel like there's a new unity surrounding me – people that care for me and love me! Someone said that I need people other than "yes men" around me. I feel really pressured by that comment. What I really, really need are friends that are really concerned for me and people that I can have a good laugh with! I need opinions, but opinions that build rather than jar. To many people, my new leadership structure looks thin, but that's because a lot of the guys have only recently "come of age". I think that it's a great team and will prove itself to be so the more we're together.

We had eight people from Kosovo in church on Sunday – all asylum seekers! Also a lady got saved on Sunday who came to the church when we began nine years ago! Amazing! I guess I can conclude that God can move on any heart and bring them to salvation. It's God who can bring people to church. It's God who can build His Church. I think we're like a space rocket that has now lost the section that used to contain the fuel used in take off – the section that helped create momentum, but is now redundant to the rest of the mission. We've been streamlined in order to get to our destination: souls and more souls.

I'm pretty weary with people transferring in from other churches. Many have been "divorced" from two or three previous churches. They carry a lot of baggage. I want souls. I need to design the church to catch as many souls as possible. I think it's the key that makes a really great church. There are a lot of people who have so much knowledge, yet their lives are so fruitless. They no longer live for the lost. God, give me good people.

On Monday I did a leaders' retreat at Milton Keynes Christian Centre. What a fantastic day it was. Good preaching, good relationship and powerful altars. The best!

27th July 2000

Two things have happened this week. We got our quotation for the work on our 700-seater auditorium. It was massive! More than anticipated. I think we'll be doing it ourselves. We won't be ready for our big conference. Secondly, one of our current tenants leasing a part of the top floor of the Megacentre is pulling out. I can't believe that so many churches work on a financial surplus. How do they do it? I'm pretty exhausted with it all.

How long Lord and how much further? We're desperate for some miracles. I know that John, our Australian builder who came over to help us, is a miracle from God. I know that our enthusiasm is a miracle. Lord, we need more, much more!

8th August 2000

We've had a fantastic last three weeks in church. The energy has increased, the numbers have been buoyant, and the preaching excellent! Certain people with particular agendas have left and it seems like the cork has been taken out of the bottle. It's August and the numbers should be down; the enthusiasm should be waning. I know that God is in on this. I declared in July that this is what I believed would happen. People are getting saved too!

I do feel like my preaching is on a higher level. I'm being myself more; I'm more relaxed; I'm more personable and more flowing! It seems that I've emerged in a new confidence. Thank you, Jesus.

22nd August 2000

All is still going great. I feel like a rocket speeding towards its destiny. God uses some people to help you get lift-off, but unless the used booster departs, it becomes a burden – everything slows and everything encumbers.

With the last evacuation of all our "super spiritual" people, I feel relief and joy. The church has experienced a dramatic increase in attendance since their departure. There's movement at the station.

On a personal note, we decided to move to a bigger house. Our house has been on the market for five days and we've had twelve couples look around and four or five offers. There's a price war on for the house. It must be the blessing of God. Three years ago we sowed part of our previous house into our building project and moved downmarket. Now the blessing of God has come to shower us with love and favour. God has shown me how He can turn situations around in power!

Even with the church's "spring clean" I've been concerned lately by a fresh couple who appeared to me to be quietly building their own kingdom. I confronted them, under wisdom from my new church advisors, and received a pretty negative reaction (at least the cards were on the table). Within three days, after some great guest ministry, we had a turn around – a complete change. My greatest pressure of last week has now been solved by God. I know that God can change hearts if people are willing. I've had a rough time, but now the blessing is coming. I've surrounded myself with friends – faithful people who carry my DNA. I feel stronger and more empowered.

26th September 2000

Our mortgage offer for our new house came through today and we're moving this Thursday. God has been so good to Jenny and me. Financially, it's a harvest time for us and I'm amazed. I've tried to buy a flat for Chris and Louise to rent cheap for a few years, but it hasn't worked out. I've tried to give money to others, but I have a suspicion that the Lord is wanting me to relax in His blessing and to note when it's the season to give and when it's the season to receive. This is a season to receive.

Some people have become acutely aware that the average age of the leadership team has severely dropped (to an average age of between 30 and 35). I've tried to redress the balance, especially by inviting two older couples onto the team, but have had no success. It must be God. It must also be a testing of the hearts of those who are worried by this. It seems that even after our recent departures, there is some new unrest starting to surface. Sometimes I wish I was more pastoral – more a big "shepherding" type. Some would say that I'm an evangelist and I lose people because of the narrowness of the gifting. I'm not sure. I know that this is all a part of a "death of the dream" test to purify my intentions and to bring my heart closer to God's heart. It seems the hardest test of all (and the one many fail in), but it's the one that will set me up for resurrection power. God just needs a good funeral!

I'm believing that out of my letting go of, and dying to my efforts to involve the over 50s, God will give us a resurrection of that age group. I'm believing that God will also give me incredibly gifted and submitted leaders that can minister to that age range.

Beside me is an incredible team. Naomi has just come from Australia and is a gift from God. Glyn is doing great and my pastoral team is so good. We're all leading with the same heart in the same direction. It should produce a blessing. Sometimes you've got to lose a few to gain a multitude.

A second minister has fallen in immorality in the past month in our city leaders' fellowship. He was part of the city leadership team that I'm on. I know that he's been off the cutting edge for some time. I'm mindful that I must keep seeking the Lord and avoid the cooling down at all costs.

Note

1. Dave Gilpin, *The Top Ten of Everything About Christian Leadership*, Monarch, 2003.

It's the 21st Century – Don't Be So Last Century

The Confusion of Style

What does church in the 21st Century look like? Many leaders across the world are looking for the answer, seeking to reinvent church to make it both potent and relevant to our world. We want a church that's inwardly intimate, yet outwardly motivated.

In this chapter, we'll be looking at how to design a church or ministry that fits the 21st Century; how to create a church geared to where the major harvest fields lie; and the top ten reasons why some churches grow and others don't.

Reinventing church for the 21st Century

The Holy Spirit is, generally, predictable. Many people expect a surprise idea from God – something new and unusual. At times, the unusual does occur, but the thing that makes it so unusual is that it is cast against the backdrop of the usual. The "usual" business of the Holy Spirit is to relay the pattern of sound teaching given through the inspired word of God. Paul writes, *"What you heard from me, keep as the **pattern** of sound teaching, with faith and love in Christ Jesus"* (2 Timothy 1:13). Patterns are repetitive arrangements of a set design. Church design in the 21st Century is still based upon a "set piece" that involves five major areas of church life.

The five zones

The role of the church is to take people from *community* to *core*. Its mission is to lead people from living with no knowledge of God to being mature disciples of Christ. The journey involves five zones of destiny:

- *Zone 1 – Community zone*
- *Zone 2 – Discovery zone*
- *Zone 3 – Foundation zone*
- *Zone 4 – Growth zone*
- *Zone 5 – Equippers zone*

Zone 1 – Community zone

This zone encompasses everything to do with our presence in the community and our cities. It includes outreach projects and personal relationships. It sows the seed of authenticity and integrity that creates listening ears. The first miracle of Jesus was to turn water into wine at a wedding. Community projects need to celebrate the great times as well as assist in the hard times in people's lives.

The first miracle of Jesus could have been to heal a hundred lepers, but He chose instead to perform a miracle not to the marginalised of society, but to the mainstream. Weddings, birthdays, and anniversaries represent the entire community and celebrate these events linking the church to those without it. Our church houses Sheffield's second largest indoor children's play centre. This is one of our flagships and in the offices behind it we care for the marginalised. What a great mix.

Many churches marginalise themselves by having a strong

community presence with marginalised groups only. People think church is for when you're down and out. Our presence needs to prove them both right and wrong!

When it comes to issues of morality and integrity, we have no right to criticise our society until we've first enhanced it. We don't *have* the right to speak, we *earn* the right to speak!

Zone 2 – Discovery zone

This zone sows the seed of our testimony. It includes personal sharing as well as evangelistic programmes. After discovering us, people now discover our story. People will firstly make decisions about *you* and then your message.

Zone 3 – Foundation zone

Here is the maternity ward of church life. It leads the new Christian along the first steps in their walk with Christ. It's done one-on-one, or facilitated by various church programmes.

Zone 4 – Growth zone

The growth zone is the zone of maturity. It's often facilitated by the main Sunday service, departmental services, and by small groups. It's also facilitated by people rubbing shoulders with each other while doing tasks together. It's where responsibilities are developed. It's all about Caanan living, not wilderness living. It's about sowing seeds, digging wells, and fighting battles.

Zone 5 – Equippers zone

This involves both leadership development and the development of teams for the overall success of the vision. It can include a partnership programme that initiates real partnering in the vision. It's vital that all five zones are vibrant and growing. Through involvement, people have a tendency towards one particular area of church life. They gravitate towards their strengths. As a leader it is essential that the chain from community to core doesn't have a weak link. The links between each zone of the journey are essential to the success of the church.

Are cells the answer?

The major key to the success in every church lies in its leadership. Leaders tend to have major strengths and non-strengths. Some will be brilliant in the community, while others excel at leading small groups. Some are pioneers, some are settlers. The idea of creating homogenous portfolios for the majority of leaders is both a daunting and unnatural task. Many cell church models are based upon the principle that all five of the zone activities are in operation in every cell. For most, that is an impossible task.

You can train your weaknesses and produce limited strength, but you will never be as strong as a person who naturally flows in their strength. To create "all-rounders" out of people who may be "half circles" will create unnecessary frustration. Every person has a strength – a God-given strength. The task of the overseer is to maximise people's strengths, create character, and manage people's weaknesses.

Cells are excellent places to encourage fellowship, discipleship, and mobilisation. Some leaders, however, who excel in events organisation (for example), fail badly when placed in other arenas. Many leaders who have a focused heart for evangelism and are placed into cell leadership produce cells that lead people to Christ, but have a very low retention factor. Again, you can train a leader in anything you like, but unless they have both eyes to see the big picture and gifting to do something about it, the results will be very limited.

The answer to the reinvented church of the 21st Century is diversity in operation – putting your best people in the community zone and your best people in each of the other four zones. Each of these people needs to be connected and empowered by both the department leaders and small group leaders.

Fathers in the faith

Another limitation of streamlining through defined "cell" groups is that the procedure can limit the number of fathers or mentors in the faith that a group member has access to. Most people are looking to find a mentor in the faith, yet Proverbs advises us that wisdom is found amongst many advisors (Proverbs 11:14). "Brothering" is the powerful advantage of small groups, but fathering is limited by them. The solution is for someone to be involved in a number of groups in the life of a church, each with another facet of fathering in operation.

The Sunday service/The living room

The prophetic word preached through a series of sermons blasts a hole through the mountains of impossibility. Evangelistic gifts lift out the fragments of rock. The pastoral strengths shape them into living stones, and the teaching strength builds in support for the newly created tunnel. The apostolic strength oversees the entire operation. It's necessary to demonstrate each of these strengths in the Sunday service.

Sunday services are the living room of the church. The living room is the place where people congregate, kick off their shoes and celebrate life. It's the place of bold declaration and great praise. It's the place of networking and fellowship. It majors on the growth zone, but also includes the foundation zone, as well as the discovery zone. It's not exclusive to one strength. It's the most popular room of the house.

Let's raise up great churches for the 21st Century that empower every zone and successfully take people from community to core.

Removing the youth annex

Most people get saved or get serious between the ages of fifteen and twenty-five. Every church that has a genuine desire for growth ought to fully resource that area of church life.

If that's where the fish are biting, simply employing a youth pastor won't cut it. Why have a church that leans towards the fifty something's, when the future is to be filled with the twenty something's? You don't want a "youth church", but you do need to have a church that's "youthy", with people of all ages totally in on the corporate venture of saving souls. Most churches begin a youth franchise by establishing a youth work that is disconnected from the main drive shaft of church life. (The franchise actually begins with the suggestion of placing an advert in a national Christian magazine before looking within the ranks of those already sown into church life.) The youth leader is eventually allowed to sit in on the elders' meetings, but the division between the in-house and the youth out-house is often exacerbated in those meetings when a tug of war on resources and direction tightens. The generation gap is exposed yet again without anyone realising that it is actually a vision gap. Youth aren't an ancillary meeting. They are the main meeting.

Vision verses style

One of the great tensions of leadership is that of pleasing everybody. It is an impossible task. Vision has built within it both a unifying factor as well as a dividing factor. Because of the open window to the young, everyone aged over forty ought to feel absolutely included in the vision of the church, if not necessarily in its style. There ought to be aspects of style that are not understood by the older generation, but accepted by them in order to outwork the vision. The vision determines the style. That's the plume in the sail of leadership. The lump in the sail of leadership is the orientation to stodgy meetings and the appeasement of stodgy people who hold on to style and glorify the past, no matter how irrelevant it may be to outreach and future growth.

The fashion cycle

Here's a case in point – I came into Christianity with *Scripture in Song* and the tunes of Dave and Dale Garrett. After singing, "You shall go out with joy" for the exhilarating millionth time, as well as its sequel, "Shine, Jesus, Shine" (shame on you for allowing your song leaders to continue to sing it; songs are like razor blades – they regularly need replacing!), we have moved on to songs that are far more complex musically, with lyrics that are less declarative and more relational. There's little Scripture in song any more. Just lately, however, I heard a batch of songs written by a new generation of twenty something's. I didn't like it – it was like a middle-aged man going back to wearing platform shoes. It was "Scripture in Song Revisited". Move with the times or the times will move without you and you'll be left with an ageing church. I'm going with the flow that's leading to the catch!

How does one create a "younger" church? Here are some clues:

▶ **1. Establish the vision.** If the fish are biting then all hands are needed. If thirteen-year-olds are getting saved by the droves, that's good for everyone. They're not youth – they're people. The vision is souls and growth. Let everything be to that aim. Eliminate ageism.

▶ **2. Encourage baton changing.** It's not jobs for life, it's vision for life. Don't let anyone hog the limelight. Form two bands from one. Start a media ministry. Add more small groups led by young people. Let your head steward be nineteen (after all, it's not rocket science to organise a meeting).

▶ *3. Engage in reinvention*. Change the way you dress and your preaching style. You may look a little silly and feel a bit uncomfortable, but it's a statement of realignment. Make sure everything you say has both a practical and prophetic edge. Banish all stodginess from your life and ministry and then be ruthless with everyone else.

▶ *4. Enrage the establishment*. Create a core team that fully imbibes the corporate vision. Add some young guns to the driving seat of the church. Provoke the sleepy and create one passionate vibrant church – not a church with an outhouse called, "Friday Youth".

▶ *5. Enter into discipleship*. Don't be intimidated by a trendy, young, enthusiastic leader. If you don't disciple him (or her), no one will. Youth leaders are prone to pick up some of the same spirits that drive the young people they are trying to reach. They need you to hone their spirit so that they don't become "one hit wonders", but get better and better as the years progress.

Some decisions are more important than others. Your decision to turn the rudder towards planet youth could be the greatest decision you ever make.

Why do some churches grow and not others?

Most of us get threatened from time to time over the growth of someone else's church or ministry. To ease the pressure, we often "box off" the other church or ministry by labelling it with a connotation that could mean underhanded leadership or easy believerism! His critics said that Spurgeon's ministry was "simply deceiving others with the deception wherewith he himself is deceived." Often, however, the true reason for criticism is intimidation and self-protection.

Church growth is what we long for and should always be the result of both the greater health of the body and the greater impact and influence on our communities. Before we look at the ten reasons why some churches grow, there are three footnotes that are the three basic habits of healthy leaders gunning for success, but not overburdened by it.

Firstly, they rejoice with those who rejoice. They don't make assumptions that could easily become rash judgements. Always remember that cynicism is the first symptom of unbelief. Thank God for another's fine work and then think little of it unless you are related in some way to it. To stare for too long at a "star" church or minister will move you from inspiration to the lust of the eyes. Lust then becomes the motivation for the new sound system and the call to evangelism.

Secondly, they realise that what they are involved in has as much value as that which others are doing. For centuries martyrs passed the baton of faith that eventually led a great outworking of the Spirit. You may be the bridge between your history and a future Wesley or Shaftsbury. Believe in your call. Each of us are called equally, "for such a time as this".

Thirdly, they realise that a lot of reasons (but not every reason) for growth are related to the quality of leadership given. Some leaders either live in denial and say, "It's all up to God," or live with constant self-annihilation as they try to live up to huge expectations that are far beyond them. Good leadership takes the right proportion of responsibility.

Now, here are ten reasons why some churches eventually grow and others don't:

▶ **1. The church is reaping the harvest of yesterday's seed.**
If you find resurrection life abounding, search back and
you'll find a funeral or a series of funerals. Someone gave
their life to the cause. If you're going through a "death"
experience, expect resurrection life to abound at a future
date. I often say that if today's church is a result of
yesterday's sowing, then the current condition of my
team's heart, mind, strength, and soul, is the guarantee of
the future condition of my church. Often, we as ministers
focus more on the outskirts of the church than the
"inskirts". It's important that we deal with causes rather
than constantly dealing with effects.

▶ **2. The church grows according to the growth of its leaders.**
Even with glitches and windfalls the church will generally
even out at the capacity of leadership. Capacity is
determined by the degree of gifting, personal maturity,
and relational maturity of the leader. As leaders grow, so
does the church. Our discipleship isn't just the transferral
of knowledge, but the transferral of the dynamic that
comes from being on a journey. Every leader must be a
pilgrim. If not, the true essence of discipleship is negated.
See to it that everyone keeps on growing.

▶ **3. The church taps into new vision.** The ability to see with
the eyes of faith and describe future possibilities is the
exclusive arena of fresh, vibrant leadership. Vision creates
motivation that is self-sustaining and self-fulfilling. On the
other hand, cynical, doubt-filled leaders invite dissent and
worldliness into the church.

▶ **4. The church no longer has a Royal family.** Immediately
after a Royal family is dethroned in any church, numbers

drop like flies. The great news is that it was the Royal family that caused the numbers to constantly hit a ceiling and then decline. With the family removed, the church can now excel beyond every previous boundary. It seems, on so many teams, that a few people set themselves up to be the "brake ministry" or the "watchmen on the walls". It can be a form of revenge or pride and needs to be revealed and dealt with.

▶ *5. The church is riding the "BIG MO".* Some churches can have a moral failure in their core team and still continue to grow. Momentum is the unseen force at work. The greater the momentum, the more unstoppable the growth. Often, bad leadership shows up twelve months after it went bad. The opposite is true too: good leadership often shows up twelve months after it went good! Success is not always related to current habits, but more so to its former habits. That leads us to our next point.

▶ *6. The church comes under apostolic leadership.* Evangelists can gather, save, motivate, and encourage. Pastors can knit, teach, nurture and support. The church can grow rapidly, but also decline rapidly without the raising up of all the "ascension" gifts from God. This is the primary role of apostolic input under which every church should shadow.

▶ *7. The church has a front door that's a little bigger than the back door.* People will always leave churches. Seed will always fall on thorny ground, even if directed to the good soil. Jesus prophesied it, so you don't have to feel condemned when it happens. A growing church has a slightly larger front door than back door. We found that for years our back door was massive. We realised that we were attracting many people of a worldly bias who were looking for personal ministry expression and these people were consistently defiling people who got to know them. When we defined our church better and the motive of all involved was more consistent with the DNA of Christ and His house, these types of people came only once or twice. They realised that they would never fit or find a place for their motivation. The result has been phenomenal – less defilement, a smaller back door and a growing congregation. Watch the little foxes that spoil the vine. Sweat the small stuff!

▶ **8. The church keeps its places to hide.** Because people are on a journey of commitment and generally paying by instalments, the layout of your church's programme should accommodate this. If the church goes solely down the track of small groups it can make the jump into church life too steep for people to traverse. Hiding places, where they can merge into the crowd, create resting places that allow people to gather their energies for another instalment of commitment to the vision of the house. This can increase the "fringe" of the church that finally increases the "core". "Community to Core" becomes a series of steps rather than one giant leap.

▶ **9. The church refuses to follow the latest fad.** Lurching is the lifestyle of a desperate leader. Strong churches keep the main thing the main thing and never get distracted by fads or momentary trends. If a leader is overly desperate to make the church grow, corners are often cut and principles abandoned. Unless new programmes are aligned to internal convictions and beliefs, they will always be short lived. Churches can become despondent when great hope has been attached to the latest programme that fails to bring growth. It comes with a guarantee, but the small print declares that it was only tried and tested in a third world country or in the USA. The location of a church warrants a tailor-made programme aligned to the God-given faith of its leadership.

▶ *10. The church has just finished a building project.* While churches raise funds for a future building, people either quietly slip away or noisily get away when they don't want to part with their money. After completion (when faith and vision have proved themselves to be true), people come from near and far through calling and fickleness! People told me that our church would grow by 20% after we moved into our new, hard-earned facilities. In fact, the church grew by 25% and continues to grow. This, though, has not always been the case. Sacrifice has kept our church lean and sleek. There will come a time when some of our current growth will leave as again we "count the cost". The great news, though, is that our future faith will be richly rewarded with increase and blessing.

Essential leadership kit
(for directions for the journey)

- Understand that the 21st Century is all about the journey of discovery. People rarely jump directly from community to core. They need a pathway.
- Create a church that's accessible to the largest harvest field – the 15 to 25s.

- Don't allow "old" people to dictate a style that they personally enjoy – it's about creating a church style that majors on saving and discipling souls.
- Know why some churches grow and others don't!

The Diary Archives

31st December 2000

This has been an awesome month. I hired a limousine and took Jenny, Colin, and Dawn, out for the night. We went to celebrate our fifteenth wedding anniversary and Dawn's thirtieth birthday. It was fantastic! We've been on holiday for two weeks in Grand Canaria, off Africa, and came back to our Christmas celebrations and more holiday! We got an offer in from the City Council to hire the top floor of the Megacentre which could be the miracle that we've been looking for. I told Glyn to call them back and try to increase the offer! I'm certain that on the basis of this leasing we can raise a massive loan and complete our plans.

We had nine people for Christmas and it took us four-and-a-half hours to unwrap all the presents! Our tradition has become to unwrap all of the presents one at a time and this year we had more than ever before – including a DVD player from the staff. We had a brilliant day.

It's almost New Year and I'm amazed at how fast the past year has gone! I feel refreshed and I'd love some new revelation from God to launch me ahead. I'm far more comfortable than ever before, though, in not having fresh revelation and not driving myself out of that state of contentment. It goes against my nature not to be constantly pushing the boundaries, but I'm learning both to trust God and to enjoy the view. I'm thanking God for all that He's done and reminding myself that He's the same God today as He always has been. I'm expecting miracles, souls, and finance, as well as incredible influence. It's been a good year. God has been gracious. Jenny and I have helped the Church of the nation move forward. Thank you Lord.

Today's update:

The deal was never followed through for the top floor. In hindsight, it would have taken up all of our parking spaces for all of our other activities. We have now turned half of the space into a conferencing centre which is hired largely by Sheffield City Council.

7th February 2001

The past year – my fortieth year – has passed so quickly. I have hardly had time to adjust to the number forty and forty-one stands just outside the door! I'm not hung up about it, but I wish I was thirty! A part of me feels like I'm ten years late in my development and fruitfulness. I'm no longer young and no longer seen as a "knight in shining armour" or even a "young rebel". I feel like I can relate much better to the "over forty" generations and I'm definitely much more confident in the business world. In public, I'm conscious of every young executive and every young 30-something minister. I can't go back and don't want to – but I would like to be younger!

Church is currently at one of those calm, almost boring, zones between one wave and the next. It's full steam ahead, yet the buzz of New Year is gone. The Visa bills from the Christmas shopping have come through the post and a subdued atmosphere pervades!

I moved away from my normal well-crafted and guarded sermons last week and let the raw side come out just to stir everyone up! It was certainly a little rough edged, but I'm desperate to lift up the people to new heights in God and get rid of the lingering atmosphere. I really dislike it when things settle and when we move back from the edge or hit some kind of ceiling.

I've been reading and studying much more than ever before. Our new house (with more rooms) is much more conducive to me working from home. I've also been enjoying books full of facts and snippets of history. I'm starting to feel quite knowledgeable.

23rd March 2001

Another month has gone by and all is quiet on the western front. Some relationships are a bit edgy and it's really difficult trying to iron things out. The hard part of being a senior minister is that you want to be best friends with those on your team, but at the same time, you want to disciple them into champions. It makes it tense at times knowing that some issues will cause temporary division. I want to address issues, but I want everyone to see a father's heart at the same time. Jenny is in Australia right now and Ryan and I have been holding the fort. Men love "cave time" and I'm no exception. I don't know if it's all that good for me to have too much. I find that I can get too melancholic for my own good if left to dwell for too long. In fact, I find it hard to construct proper sentences after a day all by myself.

This is the second month running with no baptisms. I'm disappointed and pretty stressed about it, but I do believe, however, that every church belongs to the same team and if someone else is baptising a hundred people, then it's good news for all of us. To further relieve me of my stress, I've had a revelation that my goal – my ultimate goal – isn't to bring in the harvest, but to simply please God. For me, that is at least attainable. I need to achieve and that is an attainable achievement. Reinhard Bonnke is simply pleasing God and the result is the outworking of his destiny. I can't save souls and I can't multiply finances. What I can do is put a smile on God's face and give Him great pleasure. I was reading Hebrews 11 and it appears that that was the testimony of the heroes of faith – they pleased God.

15th April 2001

Well, it's our ten year anniversary of the church. It's Easter Sunday and we had a good service this morning. Gerard Keehan came last weekend and said that there was heaps of energy in the church, but everyone seemed a bit lazy. I know what he meant. The cutting edge of evangelism has been pushed into the back-ground. The comment has really affected me and I have driven myself back again into stirring up a passion for souls. I reminded the congregation this morning that the boat we're on isn't a Caribbean cruise ship but a battleship that's running a mission for souls. I can feel that in our "overfriendliness" we have slipped off the cutting edge of our mission. We've lost our black and whiteness.

We thanked God for the first ten years and dedicated the next ten years to the cause of Christ – to seek and save people who are lost. We need to see the "Zacchaeus in the trees" and zero in on people with a persuasiveness that causes others to come out of indecision and into making a positive decision for Christ.

For the last two days I've been speaking at a church leadership conference in a town in Lincolnshire. A man with schizophrenia came up to me and said that when he gets better he wants to be a prophet. I was alarmed and said that setting up chairs and helping in the kitchen would be better and he could start now! On the second day of the conference I drove into the meeting and told Jenny that I needed a new jacket because my favourite one was starting to fall apart. At the end of the service this same man came to me and gave me a cheque for £50 for a new jacket. He knew nothing about my conversation with Jen. It was a rebuke from the Lord in the nicest possible way.

3rd May 2001

I'm sitting at Copenhagen Airport after completing my first book. I don't know whether to call it *Nonsense, Counting Chickens* or *Going Overboard*! I've got a long way to go though because it's the first draft. I've also just been to Mal Fletcher's Strategic Leadership Conference for Europe. There were around eighty people in attendance and most of them led large churches and networks. Steve Penny was there and I spent a night asking him his thoughts. I feel like the conference (and the getting away from it all) has refocused me and reinvented my thinking. Steve was saying that multi-congregations under one church was the way forward. It made me think that our heart for Manchester and Leeds could be fulfilled by incorporating them under one church. We could run a congregation in both cities and set them up just like we're set up in Sheffield. They're so close that we could provide preaching ministry each Sunday and put in place a congregational pastor. We could have a morning service in Sheffield, an afternoon service in Leeds, and a night service in Manchester! We could also expand into a Saturday night service at some stage, either in Sheffield or in another town.

My mind is racing and my heart is totally engaged! It feels like we've been in cruise mode. I think that our difficulty has been that we are apostolic, but there's been no one around to stir up the gift. We don't fit the general mould of churches. We've lived in the shadow of larger world churches and we've been waiting for our turn to see large quantities of people saved. In the meantime, I have almost let the apostolic thing cool right down. We put a stop to our reaching out to Manchester a few years ago through respect for the thoughts of one of the leaders from Hillsong Church, but I feel like we're ready to go now. I'm not a pastor or an inner city community man – I'm a church builder. It's in my blood and I know that I'm starting to rise up again to do something that's very entrepreneurial...

Today's update:
Through Steve Penny's input and inspiration we have created a multi-congregational church and are enjoying the great benefits of it. Steve leads a great multi-congregational church on the sunshine coast in Queensland and heads up the S4 network.

CHAPTER

Leaders Are Always
Between a Rock and
a Hard Place

8

The Confusion of Reality

It's a tall order to always be attempting the impossible! Church leaders are called to the extraordinary business of stepping out of the boat in anticipation of the incredible. We go far beyond what the secular business world ever does. We live in the realm of faith that exists between the "stepping out" and the "walking on"; in-between the sowing and the reaping. We are not just Sunday people, we are Saturday people – believing that Sundays are coming.

In this last chapter, we'll be looking at some final thoughts about the journey of faith and then looking at a fictitious account of the ministry from the eyes of a Reverend Bridley Jones.

The greatest challenge of leadership

Church leaders live in the fields of dreams that, in reality, are still only fields of dirt. We're called to it. We're believing for souls, maturity, influence, finance, miracles, and the leadings of God. When the crowds rejoice at answers to prayer and new signs of life, the leader has already moved on, believing for

167

more souls, more maturity ... When the path becomes a highway the leader moves out to create a new path. For the church leader who's conquered a mountain, the view back is rewarding and satisfying, but the view forward is where we're heading – to conquer another mountain. At times we'd like it to not be true, but the just shall live by faith, always!

Living by faith is both the easiest of things and the hardest of things. It's easy because faith is an absolute inner confidence that God will be all He said He would be, while He does all He said He would do. It's hard because the split second our eyes drop downwards, the sheer depth of water provokes instant doubt and fear. We are defying the gravity of popular opinion and sensible living!

Church leadership in the UK is as challenging as any nation on earth. It takes faith to believe without seeing for indefinite periods of time. While churches in other nations see truck loads of souls being saved on a daily basis, our challenge is to stay in the zone of believing. That's a real challenge!

I am always perplexed by the question, "How's things?" What do you say? "How's **things** meant to be?" I have wondered why I am so often between a rock and a hard place! Is there something wrong with me? Shouldn't I be flourishing on every side with a great looking church, great family, great car and great friends? I have concluded that, maybe, things are the way they are, not because I'm in the wrong place because of unbelief, but because I'm actually in the right place. It's faith that has driven me into the middle of a valley. Faith loves to go there! That's where faith comes into its own and latches onto the miracle power of heaven.

How's things? Belligerent! How am I? Buoyant, bold, and bright. The two responses point simultaneously to two opposing landscapes. My inner world is like the Welsh valleys – calm and tranquil (well, within reason!). My outer world stares at a void, ready to be confronted and filled by extracts from heaven. Sometime soon everything will start to come together. That's why you can't tell a "man of faith" by the car he drives or the house he owns. You can't tell a "woman of faith" by the size of the ministry she runs or by the number of friends that she has. You just can't tell! If anything, the only indication of faith in a leader's life is the mountains he/she confronts and the spirit he/she exudes. Faith is divorced from circumstances and only attached to the unseen world of tomorrow. The moment faith achieves the impossible and you stand on the mountain of success, you can't stay there. Success doesn't need faith! When a life is a continuous life of faith we're always taken from fullness to emptiness. It's God's fodder for a future harvest.

Bridley Jones' Diary (BJD)

In an attempt to bring a little humour into the life of leadership, I've invented the diary of a Reverend Bridley Jones. Many of the challenges that you face are also faced by a multitude of leaders across the country, including Rev. Bridley! The journey of faith can become pretty intense. These diary extracts are designed to bring some light relief to your calling into leadership.

Reverend Jones has been the Rector of St Titus for five long years. He knows that he's been called "for such a time as this", but is wondering if he's been called "for such a place as this". He loves some of the people all of the time and all of the people some of the time. Anyhow . . . here are some snippets from his most intimate thoughts.

Sunday 30th November (BJD)
It crossed my mind to check if the tape I chose to play after the communion message had been cued correctly. I finished my spiel about the power of the cross and then silence. Looking for

a seamless continuation of mood from the spoken words to the introduction of the song I'd spent an hour trying to find, all we heard was the sound guy scrambling around for the tape that was handed to him just before the service by a friend of the secretary. I could feel my secret vendetta against the sound ministry rise again to an all too familiar level. When the tape finally started to roll I gave a casual, but loaded, glance to the back of the hall and I think he got the message. The only problem is that he sent me back a little look and I think he was delivering mail as well! Even though I know that by tomorrow I will have cooled slightly, I couldn't help being disheartened by the foiling of another great plan through ineptitude.

Why is it that I'm the only one who seems to care? Am I just really pedantic or is there simply no one around to lift up my arms like they did to Moses and like they do to that guy at the Christian Centre in town. Why am I the abandoned one? After the service finished I still felt pretty hard done by, but I managed to leave a little earlier than normal without sharing it with anyone. I had preached well and soon that will be my predominant thought.

While driving home I felt in a real tussle. Should I ask my wife what she thought of my excellent exposition of Paul's theology on suffering, or shall I wait for a spontaneous outburst of praise? After all, if she'd liked it, I'd enjoy the praise better if it wasn't extracted from her, but was freely and naturally given. Silence. I waited, not wanting to clog the air with any other agenda. More silence. I couldn't wait any longer so I ducked around to the back door of her thoughts to try to get an agreement on how bad the sound guy was. She reckoned that she didn't even notice! I told her that I'd like to sack him, but after quickly calculating the collateral damage (his mum is the only piano player as well as bridge partner of one of the Elders' wives), I decided to let ineptitude rule for just one more week.

In a desperate measure that seemed to come from an insatiable need to be affirmed, I finally asked my wife, "How do you think I went?" I needed more, much more, than "Good". I'd been up till 1.00am preparing my message and I knew that I'd nailed it. I just needed to know that I'd nailed it. "You did great," was her three word response – an extracted response. Was she saying only what I wanted to hear? Why do I feel depressed after doing so well?

I ran through the morning's attendance, engrossing me so that even the question of, "What would you like for lunch?" went completely unheard. Overall, after including the two stewards just outside the hall and the possibility of one or two people using the toilets at any one given time, the tally seemed a little down. I emerged from my sea of thought and asked my wife what she thought about the numbers. She thought the congregation had looked a little bigger. I felt much, much better. My mind switched to that little group that seems to coagulate in the corner of the hall while everyone else is circulating around tea and coffee after the service has finished. They seem nice enough, but I'm worried. They seem pretty spiritual – almost too spiritual.

I noticed a lot of "laying on of hands" going on. I believe in it, but isn't there a time and a place for it? And why did I feel excluded when I went within five yards of "the club"? I'm the Pastor! It smells like a franchise ministry setting out its stall. What can I do? I felt pretty helpless and decided to call one of my leaders to keep an eye on the matter. He told me that the ring leader has recently come from St Mark's and caused some trouble there. Why wasn't I warned? I think that maybe I should really pray about it, but in the meantime I find it quite easy to decide the content of next Sunday's message.

After lunch I read through the Sunday papers and once again noticed the "Appointments" section. I'm not looking for another job, but I've been doing some comparisons to see what the going rates are nowadays. What's the equivalent job to a Minister of Religion? I went for Regional Sales Manager of a drinks company. Searching through the small print I found what I have known to be the truth ever since I arrived at St Titus: I'm underpaid ... big time.

Thinking of the money I could now be on if I'd stayed on in my secular job, I felt not only undervalued, but also a bit used. Well .... very used. I hoped that someone from my salaries committee would glance through the same "careers section" and see how much wages have gone up in the past few decades. To ever replace me would be costly, I'm sure.

Monday 1st December (BJD)

Sleep in. Yes! I woke to the sound of the vacuum cleaner that seemed to have an amplifier attached. I opened my eyes to a visual demonstration of "a woman's work is never done", presented directly before me. Feeling slightly condemned I got up and made the bed. Feeling quite proud of making amends so quickly I headed downstairs for a well deserved cup of coffee and felt a little extra "buzz" kicking in. I did preach well yesterday. It's a shame none of my minister colleagues know how good I actually am. Whenever they've heard me I've always been a tad nervous which has affected the overall flow, and flow is important. If only they could have seen me. Maybe news will spread and I may be "in demand" one day. The only problem with doing so well is that you've got a lot to live up to the following Sunday. I contemplated the added pressure and it's that added pressure that will virtually prevent me from being any good the next time. That is a perfect Catch 22: a perfectly bad one.

My wife asked me if I wanted to go shopping and my reluctant response caused a momentary loss of Christian virtue.

Amongst the rapid fire I caught the deliberately mean and callous statement, "Well, it looks like you love the church more than you love me." "What is love?" I mused defensively after producing the necessary white flag. Why is it that in every argument I'm always the one in the wrong and always the one who's first to say "sorry"? I thought over the past few battles and contemplated the impossibility of always been in the wrong. Surely there's one fight where I was well justified? I decided wisely to keep those particular thoughts to myself, but did note that next time it's her turn to say sorry first, if for the sake of justice only!

Met a woman at the shopping mall who recognised me, but I couldn't for the life of me remember her name. I asked her how long she'd been attending St Titus and she said for around a year. I tried to hide my embarrassment by looking overly surprised at how quickly time flies. My mention of the fact that it seemed only yesterday that Princess Diana tragically died, brought a sobering diversion to the fact that I barely recognised the woman in front of me. Did she attend weekly? Did she leave immediately after the conclusion of each of the services? Was I losing a vital part of my memory? Did I honestly care on my one day off? I did and I didn't. She seemed likeable and I said that I'd chat to her on Sunday.

My wife returned from the department store and I took an interest in her purchases. I was amazed at her pleasure in my interest and instantly recalled the part of the marriage seminar that talked about investing into your spouse's emotional bank account. Invest I did and a sense of delight was felt all around. I did wonder, though, if my investing was part of an underlying strategy for future transactions the other way. Later, with my wife asleep early and the bank now well and truly closed, I stayed up late trying to catch the last minutes of freedom before the next day's 7.00–8.00am Intercessory Revival Glory prayer meeting was upon me. Maybe tomorrow would be a new day and the prayer meeting would be really full. I slept well under that little ray of sunshine, only occasionally rewinding in my mind the clever interweaving of deep truth with strands of hearty humour in my Pauline discourse. Many call me Pastor, but I get the feeling that there may be more to me than that. Surely I could be veering into the prophetic or even entering the powerful domain of "apostlehood"? Maybe . . . just maybe.

Tuesday 9th February (BJD)

I spent the morning feeling a little tired but upbeat! With a 20% increase in the "Revival Glory" early morning prayer attendance, we could all tangibly feel the presence of God in the room. We had some really encouraging prophecies about our town being the epicentre of a coming revival and it made me feel all tingly. Everyone hung around just that little bit longer and they all said that they felt full of faith. After chatting to the hangers on, I went straight to my office, shut the door, and relaxed in my new swivel chair from Ikea (just enough spring action to kick back without toppling!). What should I do now? I put my hands behind my head and savoured the moment. I felt really important. I made sure I had my Bible and my Pukka pad open just in case someone popped in without knocking. I didn't want to look like I hadn't got enough to do. How many would turn up next week? I decided not to get overly excited, but after reading *The Tipping Point* recently, I've got a feeling we may have just tipped over into the beginnings of who knows what!

Tuesday 16th February (BJD)

Depressed. "Revival Glory" isn't living up to its name. We had a prophecy that we were facing the southern gate of the demonic realm and that Satan's powers were advancing (I could only think of the Orks amassing on the plains of Middle Earth). It felt

like our prayers were hitting the ceiling and then falling hope-
lessly to the ground. None of us felt the presence of God. All five
others left immediately after I said, "Amen". I slumped into my
new chair and contemplated how hard it is being a Minister.

Why, just why, can't we grow like St Barnabas? What's
wrong with us? I picked up the "Barna Buzz" newsletter of
St Barnabas and it really annoyed me to see the band and
hundreds of people worshipping God. They looked so happy
and so young! Everyone is good looking. I think they might also
have two projectors on the ceiling. I can't stand it any more. It
must be so easy for them. I wondered if their church was just a
"preaching centre" and then said sorry to God for going along
that line of thought.

Friday 19th February (BJD)

Message preparation day. I like Friday: no people to see, no
places to go. It's not that I don't love people, it's just that it's
great to have a break. I felt happier – just me and some paper.
What should I speak on this Sunday? It's always easier when I'm
doing a series. The last series on the "Be happy-tudes" went
down really well. I looked back through my quiet time notes to
get a clue for Sunday – thought they might trigger something. I
calculated that I've preached over two-hundred and forty-six
times at St Titus. No wonder it's hard to think up what to
preach on next. I wondered if Yonggi Cho was in my place,
whether he'd have a church of thousands, or if the problem is
just with the people. They just don't get it! Is it worth me
sowing my life into all these people when not a lot seems to be
happening?

Ralph from "Eagle's Nest" reckons that there's a spiritual
stronghold over the area that's stopping us all flourishing. He
says that if we get all the churches together then the devil will
be pushed back. He's got his church praying over the four gates

of the town. I'm a bit miffed at Ralph and can't see all that stuff in the Bible – but I could be miffed because a couple have started going to his church from ours and they don't like me because I refused to "send" them on their way. I hate to be hated. Maybe I should just have been nice and given them my blessing?

I decided to do an oldie but goodie. I wondered if I was just getting slack, but consoled myself with the thought that it might actually be what God wants for this coming Sunday. Why preach "new" when they haven't got the "old"? I call my wife to see if she remembers the "axe-head" sermon. She doesn't. Hurrah! We just found out that our cat has lost all but three of its teeth. They must have fallen out and none of us knew about it. I'm going to use that for my intro and tell them they could have lost their cutting edge without knowing about it too. I congratulated myself on my cleverness with a coffee and a penguin. Fresh intro, fresh ending ... solid word. God is good!

Sunday 21st February (BJD)

"Running out of material" was the *last* comment I wanted to hear after the service. I laughed it off, but was mad. "If you kept your cutting edge and didn't lose it so often, Buddy, I wouldn't have to speak to you about it again!" I refrain from saying anything. "Easier to cut off a head than sew it back on" a wise man once said!

I didn't know if Ralph's spirits were getting really stirred today, but the service was hard from beginning to end. My worship leader sang a "Hillsong" then "When I survey" and, as predicted, the volume of the congregation rose noticeably for the hymn. I figure that it's nostalgia over things that have been going for much longer than we have. While we were in worship I glanced around with my hands in the air and saw five people sitting down looking bored. Why did they even bother to come this morning if they couldn't be bothered to do a simple thing like standing up? I wondered if that was a "religious spirit" in me. I figured out it's better in future to turn a blind eye, and better still not even to look back to see what's really going on. I guess the worship did go on for a longer time than usual. It was really heavy going.

Phil, our worship leader, didn't seem his normal self today. Even though I've told him how much I love the new "Majesty" song, he still hasn't included it in any of the services in the past two months. Maybe I shouldn't worry about it. After all it's not all about me. He does drag the songs out though . . . I'm reticent to tell him because a year ago he got a bit shirty when I told him that I didn't want him to wear jeans with rips in them while leading worship. I'm not good at confrontation, so I decide this time not to bring anything up. If he throws in the towel who else have I got? I decide to go for the easy option and put it all in God's hands.

As usual at 10.46am we had a prophecy from Mrs Kerslake (well, it doesn't happen every week, but fairly often). She says some good things, but usually seems to leave a "not so good" feeling in the air. I know it's "a new season" and that "a good clean out" is important, but instead of lifting the people it just seemed to make them more dreary. Dreary I hate. I talked with her after the service and found out that she still regularly sees the couple that are now at Ralph's "Eagle Nest" church. Too regularly for comfort. It's not that I don't want inter-church fellowship, but birds of a certain feather flock together, even if they are in different flocks. What bugs me is that slight air of superiority she exudes, as if she knows something I don't. Maybe she does . . . she seems to "feel it" much more than me. I tried to give her the benefit of the doubt, but the doubt is really running out of benefit!

We tried out the new lapel microphone today and upon my entry to the pulpit I tried all the switches, but no sound availed. Even though everyone could hear me without it I still felt stupid tapping it and saying, "Can you hear me?" over and over. The sound man realised that he hadn't put the new batteries in it and strolled up with the Ever Ready's in hand. I tried to look cool, but underneath my blood was starting to boil. My chance at being Mr Motivator was now being stolen from me. I resisted eye contact and made a joke of it, but not many people laughed. When the service had finished (and after someone gave me that derogatory comment about running out of material) I headed down the aisle and almost ran past the sound desk. Why can't they just get it? What's so hard about making sure the microphone is going to work? And why does the sound vary so much from week to week? Can't they just leave the dials alone? A friend of mine said that women make much better sound men than men because men love to fiddle. How true it is.

Next Sunday we have a special guest speaker, Alvin Starman (the Very Reverend). I get really nervous when guests come. I hope it's nothing like today has been. He used to be a visiting speaker at the church I grew up in. I decided to write to everybody during the week to ensure that they come on Sunday. At night I thanked God for His goodness to me and for getting me through another day, despite it being hard. I know that Jesus went through it all and so shall I. I took comfort from that thought and escaped into Midsummer Murders. Thank you Lord.

Wednesday 7th May (BJD)
The telephone woke me up and I looked at the alarm clock. 8.45am. Oops, I'd slept in again. I cleared my voice as much as I could and answered with a sprightly, but rather croaky, "Hello,

Bridley speaking." "Did I wake you up?" Drat! What do you say when you're suddenly confronted by the one question you wanted to avoid? "No, no – just a little cold I think." I started to feel bad at the white lie. A little white lie – an itsy bitsy untruth – no matter how I say it, still makes me feel bad. What would Alan think if he knew that I'd been woken up from a long night's sleep by his call at almost nine o'clock in the morning?

Elder Alan has quite an influence. I decided to carry the dark deception throughout the length of our conversation. I think I'm a little bit afraid of him. I've known him ever since I was called to St Titus, but I've never been able to relax when he's been in the same room. I never feel like he's on quite the same page as me. I know I'm accountable to him and I feel like he knows it too, and plays with me like a cat with a mouse. I don't like it. Every time I suggest something in our team meetings, he waits until the conversation starts to die down and everybody's had their say and then adds his bit. Why couldn't he just join in when everybody was joining in? He's like a wise owl that peers down until everyone says their tuppence worth, then he speaks his grand wisdom, glaring through the lower glass of his bifocals. After informing me that he'd like some more information on office spending, we said goodbye. I immediately walked downstairs in my pyjamas to offload to my wife. "I hate Alan," is the expression I mostly use.

Thursday 8th May (BJD)

Spent half an hour meditating on our cell groups. I was feeling like a name change is in order. If my neighbours find out that I run cells they may think I'm up to something. With the rise of Muslim fundamentalism (with the emphasis on the mental), they may even think I have something to do with sleeper cells. I gave a little chuckle as I thought about how many sleepy cells

I actually oversee. Still, I don't want a visit from under-cover officers.

I took a phone call from Nicola down at the church. She said that one of the cell leaders wanted to see me. I immediately asked her, "Are you sure? Did he tell you what it would be about?" I started to feel my blood pressure increase. Nicola told me about the need for a second computer in the office and the possibility of an upgrade to Pentium II, but being otherwise engaged in deep forensic detective work, she left the conversation for a more opportune time. Why would George want to see me? He has had his arms folded the last two times I've preached and he has started to sit down during the slow worship songs. I was worried. Most people who want to see me have bad news. Maybe he's leaving? I've heard that he's still friends with Fran and Diane who have recently taken "time out" of their heavy church schedule, but were seen up at St Chad's last Sunday. I told Nicola to arrange the meeting ASAP.

Friday 9th May (BJD)

I couldn't concentrate any more. The tension was getting to me. I waited at my desk for a knock on the door. I offered George a coffee, but he refused. After small talk about the worldwide terrorists threats and the menace of disaffected terror cells (and their leaders), I asked him how he was doing. He told me he was a bit unhappy with things and knew a lot of other people who were as well. I asked him for names but he insisted, "It's a lot." I pushed the envelope (which is not like me), but he said he couldn't break the special trust that the others had placed in his confidence. I braced myself. He told me that the anointing seemed to have lifted off me, as well as off the worship. He said he didn't get much satisfaction from the services anymore and there was general dissatisfaction with the vision. I went into defence mode and told George that I was trying to make the church more "user friendly". I think George is more "Hinn" than "Hybels". More "Wagner" than "Warren". He still had his arms folded. He told me that he'd leave it with me and I cringed at the challenge while trying to look un-phased.

Upon his swift exit I quickly computed the damage. I went through the cell report and found that he hadn't filled one in for the past two months. I asked Nicola (because she knows everything) about who went to his cell and she ticked off the names of five people who attended on a regular basis. What to do ... if he leaves, they'll all leave. I could feel myself knotting up. There are bills to pay and we're already sailing close to the wind. The second computer will have to wait until fairer weather. I asked God why pastoring is so difficult and decided one day to write a leadership book called, *Jesus, Save Me from My Followers*.

Saturday 10th May (BJD)

I think I lost the will to fight. I prayed a small prayer for the "uprising" and handed the situation over to the sovereignty of God, only to take it back again five minutes later. Why can't church life be easy for a change? This kind of thing never seems to happen to anyone else. What is it about my leadership that's missing? Sure, I'm not charismatic like Chris at City Life, and I'm not as knowledgeable as J. C. Thornton at St Oswald's. Am I really cut out for this? I thought about what other profession I'd do if I vacated myself from the ministry. I got even more depressed when I started thinking about the reduced employment opportunities for the middle aged. What have I really achieved in my lifetime? My wife told me to let it go. She reminded me of my message only two weeks ago entitled, "Called". She can be really annoying when I'm in a sulk.

Friday 16th May (BJD)

I'm mad. Wayne Walker from St Chad's hasn't had the courtesy to ask me about the leakage from our church to his. Maybe he believes all the stuff that they're saying about me. I feel like my reputation may be taking a tumble (yet again). Wayne knows a lot of people and to him it probably looks like our church is falling apart. There's something about St Chad's that I don't like. I reminded myself only eight people have left in total. I added it up again. Only eight. With two young people getting saved last Sunday, it's only a dip of six. I decided to revisit past prophecies. That made me feel better, but what's the big delay? From somewhere across the road from my office, I heard the doleful melody of the song, "A Long and Winding Road". The devil is out in force today.

Essential leadership kit (to stay true on the journey)

- Living by faith doesn't mean you drive a fabulous car and have an ever-growing church.
- Faith takes you into the impossible because it has a power to unlock. If you're in a desert, something's about to happen.
- There's an insecure and fed-up "Bridley" inside every one of us. Part of staying sane is knowing you're not alone.

The Diary Archives

28th May 2004

The last three years have been good years in the life of Hope City Church. All of my leaders have grown stronger and wiser and we have now become a multi-congregational church with congregations in Sheffield, Manchester, and Liverpool. Hopefully, we'll be adding Leeds in late October. Our overall Sunday attendance is around 800 people and our goal is to reach 1,000 by the end of 2004.

Last year, we only kept one in every three of our new converts and it's our aim this year to keep at least two out of three. It's a big challenge, but a necessary one.

Glyn is seeing great fruit with National Youth Ministry and it has necessitated a reinvention of the way we oversee our church departments. Jenny is going great with the "Fabulous You" women's conference and network and at some stage we'll definitely need an overseeing pastor to help us with the growth of our main Sheffield congregation.

I still get affected greatly by people who leave the church and especially those who gave no signs that their departure was looming. I suspect that there's much going on in people's lives that I know nothing about (because of their inability to open up and really share what's going on).

God has really helped us financially and we have continued to push the boat out with each fresh gust of faith. We were right on the wire three months ago and after bringing it to the "Partners in the Vision", we were able to recover £30,000 and pay every outstanding invoice. It certainly opened the eyes of our partners to the enormity of the task at hand and I think that God had His hand on the way the provision was provided for.

Our Liverpool congregation came about through the part adoption of a small congregation that had at one stage been a much larger influence in the city. It hasn't been an easy change over, but we're certain that we'll see a thriving expression of Hope City Church in Liverpool. Our Manchester congregation began just with myself and a great team from Sheffield and we recently moved it from Sunday nights to Sunday morning and withdrew a large part of the team. It's going great and has a buzz that is infectious. It's our heart to keep it all one church and the advantages of this corporative-ness are completely evident in every area of our church life.

Well, here's to the future! It's in God's hands already and my "confidence" scripture is from Psalm 138: *"The LORD will fulfil his purpose for me."* God will do it. It's His purposes and not mine. It's in the bag.

Today's update:

We now have four congregations across the north of England with the addition of our Leeds congregation. The Liverpool church, that we partly adopted to form the beginning of Hope City Church, Liverpool, has reappeared in Liverpool with its old name intact and with many of the original people (led by its former assistant minister). We've just started to see a thousand different people come through our doors on Sunday and have started a special multi-media, evangelistic meeting every Sunday night in Sheffield to help accomplish this dream.

I feel like my life has hit a new season of freedom and freshness as I explore my freshly discovered creative streak! Somehow I feel like I'm finally off the foundations both personally and as Senior Pastor of Hope City Church. It's taken forever, so I'm savouring the season!

About the Author

Dave Gilpin is Senior Pastor of Hope City Church which has congregations in Sheffield, Liverpool, Manchester and Leeds. He also heads up a leadership network in the UK called S4 and is author of *SQ: Boost your Spiritual IQ*, *The Top 10 of Everything About Christian Leadership* and *Rage against Beige*.

Dave was born in 1960 in Clatter Bridge Hospital, Bebbington. At the age of five his family moved to Brisbane then to Melbourne, finally ending up in Canberra, Australia. Dave left home to complete a Civil Engineering degree at Sydney University. It was in his third year at University that he became a Christian through a large evangelistic push called, "Know Christ, Know Life; No Christ, No Life". He realised that the emptiness within him was in the shape of God and could be filled by Him alone.

After two years working for a concrete company as a plant manager, Dave attended Renewal Ministry Training College in Brisbane in order to strengthen his walk with God and explore God's plan for his life. After college, Dave became the Youth Pastor at Southside Christian Renewal Centre and was then sent out to fulfil his vision for the UK.

As well as leading Hope City Church Dave also oversees the Megacentre, which is a conferencing and community centre, as well as the operations centre for the church. Dave is married to Jenny and they have one son called Ryan, who was born in the same year that Hope City Church began. He has also recently discovered the joy of painting and signs all of his paintings "Dagarté"! He thinks that it has a better ring to it than "Dave"!

We hope you enjoyed reading this New Wine book.
For details of other New Wine books
and a range of 2,000 titles from other
Word and Spirit publishers visit our website:
www.newwineministries.co.uk